Redefining the Discipline of Adult Education

Robert D. Boyd
Jerold W. Apps
and Associates

Redefining the Discipline of Adult Education

374
R314

Jossey-Bass Publishers

San Francisco • Washington • London • 1980

REDEFINING THE DISCIPLINE OF ADULT EDUCATION
by Robert D. Boyd, Jerold W. Apps, and Associates

Jossey-Bass Inc., Publishers
433 California Street
San Francisco, California 94104

Jossey-Bass Limited
28 Banner Street
London EC1Y 8QE

Library of Congress Cataloging in Publication Data

Main entry under title:

Redefining the discipline of adult education.
   (Adult Education Association handbook series in
adult education)
   Bibliography: p. 190
   Includes index.
   1.   Adult education—Addresses, essays, lectures.
I.   Boyd, Robert Dean, 1916–   II.   Apps,
Jerold W., 1934–   III.   Series: Adult Education
Association.   Adult Education Association handbook
series in adult education.
LC5219.R42   374   80-8006
ISBN   0-87589-482-8

Manufactured in the United States of America

JACKET DESIGN BY WILLI BAUM

FIRST EDITION

Code 8043

The AEA Handbook Series
in Adult Education

WILLIAM S. GRIFFITH
University of British Columbia

HOWARD Y. McCLUSKY
University of Michigan

General Editors

Edgar J. Boone
Ronald W. Shearon
Estelle E. White
and Associates
Serving Personal and
Community Needs Through
Adult Education

April 1980

John M. Peters
and Associates
Building an Effective
Adult Education
Enterprise

April 1980

Huey B. Long
Roger Hiemstra
and Associates
Changing Approaches
to Studying Adult
Education
April 1980

Alan B. Knox
and Associates
Developing, Administering,
and Evaluating
Adult Education
October 1980

Robert D. Boyd
Jerold W. Apps
and Associates
Redefining the Discipline
of Adult Education
October 1980

Foreword

Adult education as a field of study and of practice is not well understood by many literate and intelligent American adults whose exposure to the field has been limited to one or a few aspects of its apparently bewildering mosaic. Since 1926, when the American Association for Adult Education (AAAE) was founded, the leaders of that organization and its successor, the Adult Education Association of the U.S.A. (AEA), have striven to communicate both to the neophytes in the field and to the adult public an understanding of its diverse and complex enterprises. A major vehicle for accomplishing this communication has been a sequence of handbooks of adult education, issued periodically to convey a broad view of the mosaic. In 1934, 1936, and 1948 the AAAE published the first three handbooks. Although the Association had intended to issue a handbook every two years, that plan was not carried out for a number of reasons, including the outbreak of World War II and the termination of support by the Carnegie Corporation. Within three years of the publication of the 1948 handbook the Association itself dissolved in order to establish the AEA, which included the former members of both the AAAE and the Department of Adult Education of the National Education Association. It was nine years before the AEA was able to publish its first handbook, the fourth in the sequence, followed a decade later by the fifth version.

In the early 1970s both the Publications Committee of AEA and the Commission of the Professors of Adult Education (an affiliated organization of the AEA) explored the kinds of handbooks that could be designed to serve the changing nature and needs of the field. They found that different parts of the field were developing at different rates—in some areas information was becoming outdated rapidly, whereas in others a decennial handbook would be adequate to maintain currency. Moreover, the growing literature and the many developments in policies and programs led them to conclude that a single volume of traditional size would not be sufficient to treat the expanding knowledge base, the changing policies and practices, and the controversial topics in adult education. Accordingly, the Publications Committee decided that the next handbook would consist of several volumes, allowing the presentation of an increased amount of information on each of nine selected parts of the field and preparing the way for subsequent revisions of each volume independently on a schedule reflecting the pace of change in each area. The result is The AEA Handbook Series in Adult Education, which is being developed by the general editors with the guidance and assistance of the Publications Committee.

Redefining the Discipline of Adult Education is a successor to *Adult Education: Outlines of an Emerging Field of University Study* and a part of the series which succeeds the 1970 *Handbook of Adult Education in the United States.* In this book Boyd and Apps, who served as organizers of the volume, express the view that students of adult education have borrowed rather indiscriminately from other disciplines. The result, they contend, is that the scholarly literature is inadequately integrated and poorly linked with practice. They are attempting through the presentation and application of their model to the field of practice to demonstrate how knowledge can be classified and integrated and how its development can be accelerated. Their criticisms of the work of some adult education scholars may be misread as an ill-conceived rejection of all concepts and theories from the other social sciences. Further reflection by the reader will lead to the conclusion that they do not oppose borrowing, but rather argue for wiser borrowing from other disciplines.

Eight other volumes together with *Redefining the Discipline of Adult Education* make up the Handbook Series in Adult Education. The other eight deal with research, the organization of adult education, managing adult learning experiences, program areas, current issues, training, comparative adult education, and adult education administration.

Preparation of the series required the cooperation and dedicated efforts of scores of chapter authors, Publication Committee chairmen and members, and successive executive committees of the AEA. In bringing together the insights and perceptions of adult education scholars, the series is a major contribution of the Association to the advancement of an understanding of adult education as a field of study and of practice.

September 1980   WILLIAM S. GRIFFITH
                                                    HOWARD Y. McCLUSKY

                                                    General Editors

Preface

In the first chapter of this book, the senior authors present a descriptive and conceptual paradigm of adult education as a field of study and of practice. Our associates were asked to consider this paradigm as a reference point for their discussions of specific forms of adult education. Thus, although the paradigm occupies a central role, this volume is an anthology of conceptual views of the foundations of adult education.

We had several primary objectives when we began this project. We accepted the challenge proferred by Jensen, Liveright, and Hallenback in their *Adult Education: Outlines of an Emerging Field of Study* (1964), that adult educators construct a conceptual framework to demarcate the practice and study of adult education.

A second objective was to structure this volume as an integrated inquiry. All contributing authors were asked to explain their fundamental positions in their area of expertise and to alert the reader to foundational issues. To emphasize these issues and to point out conflicts among the authors, we have annotated the text, using end-of-chapter notes to address differences in foundational positions.

We expected and encouraged criticisms and questions about the adequacy and usefulness of our paradigm. We hope that the reader will find such expressions of foundational differences both informative and provocative. Our intention is that this volume stimulate serious discussion among professionals.

   We present our paradigm in Chapter One. The remainder of the volume is divided into four parts. Part One contains two chapters on the adult as an independent learner. Part Two comprises three chapters that examine the group mode of adult education. Part Three, five chapters devoted to community adult education, is the largest segment of the volume because we felt that this aspect of adult education required the most extensive examination. Part Four contains a critique of the conceptual foundations presented in this volume and our response to that critique.

Madison, Wisconsin   ROBERT D. BOYD
September 1980   JEROLD W. APPS

Contents

The Authors

JEROLD W. APPS, professor, Department of Continuing and Vocational Education, University of Wisconsin, Madison

ROBERT D. BOYD, professor, Department of Continuing and Vocational Education, University of Wisconsin, Madison

PATRICK G. BOYLE, professor, Division of Program and Staff Development, University of Wisconsin Extension, Madison

M. DONALD CAMPBELL, specialist, Office of Continuing Education and Public Service, University of Illinois, Urbana-Champaign

ROBERT A. CARLSON, professor and chairperson, Continuing Education Program, University of Saskatchewan, Saskatoon

CHERE C. COGGINS, assistant professor and program specialist, University of Minnesota Extension, St. Paul

LYNN E. DAVIE, associate professor, Department of Adult Education, Ontario Institute for Studies in Education, Toronto

MICHAEL G. MOORE, senior counsellor, Open University—Southern Region, Oxford, England

RUSSELL D. ROBINSON, professor, Department of Educational Administration and Supervision, University of Wisconsin, Milwaukee

ALLEN TOUGH, associate professor, Department of Adult Education, Ontario Institute for Studies in Education, Toronto

JOHN P. WILSON, associate professor, extension specialist in Adult Education, Iowa State University, Ames

JOAN W. WRIGHT, associate professor, Department of Adult and Community College Education, North Carolina State University at Raleigh

Redefining the Discipline of Adult Education

Chapter One

A Conceptual Model
for Adult Education

Robert D. Boyd

Jerold W. Apps

This book is organized on the premise that adult education has its own unique structure and function. The format of this volume is unlike many foundation books, as it is not primarily a compilation of research literature. Rather, this book is the result of a project to define the conceptual foundations of adult education.

This chapter presents a model for conceptualizing adult education. First, we argue the need for such a model for adult education as a field of study and practice. Second, we formally describe the model and present illustrative examples.

Several authorities in adult education have offered definitions of adult education. Schroeder (1970) reviews many of these definitions, some of which propose a conceptual framework within which to view adult education, while others delineate characteris-

1

tics by which to define adult education. Jensen (1964) describes adult education as being built upon experience "gained from coping with problems of practice [that] lead to the formulation of principles" (p. 105). He proposes that adult education borrow and reformulate knowledge developed by other disciplines. We shall point out in this chapter certain serious problems associated with such borrowing of knowledge. Boyd (1966) provides a conceptualization of adult education from a psychological perspective, but his formulation is limited to the learner's orientation in adult education. Our review of the literature thus provided no approach similar to the direction we are here proposing. Our present efforts lead in a direction that has not as yet been explored.

The first principle that distinguishes our theory from others is that we believe it is an error to seek assistance from recognized disciplines until we have clearly understood the structure, function, problems, and purposes of adult education itself. Only then is it appropriate to seek assistance in solving problems and answering questions. An example may clarify this point. Consider an adult educator who is reading a psychologist's studies on anxiety. The adult educator sees what he believes to be striking similarities between the psychologist's accounts and observations he has made in his classroom.* Assuming the material to be suitable, he removes it from its given context and places it in another. It appears to fit, and this appearance seems to afford legitimacy to his appropriation. In point of fact, the two contexts may not be isomorphic and, therefore, much confusion and even improper action may result from such borrowing of concepts and research findings.

There are two arguments against this free borrowing of concepts and theories. First, before we seek help from other disciplines, we must clearly see the unique and particular configurations of adult education as an activity. Second, before borrowing material, we must establish the similarities and dissimilarities between the context of that material and our own context. We must ask ourselves what erroneous assumptions we may be accepting

* The traditional use of the pronoun *he* has not yet been superseded by a convenient, generally accepted pronoun that means either *he* or *she*. Therefore, the authors use *he* while acknowledging the inherent inequity of the traditional preference of the masculine pronoun.

when we borrow from established disciplines to define problems in adult education. When scholars define the nature of and solutions to problems in their field of study, they are defining that field of study, its premises, mode of argumentation, and criteria for proof. But the methodology of the social and natural sciences are not necessarily appropriate to the problems of adult education.

We have identified four erroneous assumptions that proponents of borrowing from other disciplines have taken for granted. First, that concepts from other disciplines can be applied directly to adult education without specifying situational variables. Direct appropriation is an error because the disciplines, usually seen as sources of concepts for adult education, developed their concepts without concern for adult education. We argue for the importance of context; that is, the influence of existing forces in a given situation are important determinants of that situation. We are suspicious of any findings that do not share situational variables with the problem we are investigating. The expression of tension in a classroom may be anxiety as defined and explored by psychologists in their studies, but until the dynamics of the classroom and the setting studied by psychologists are shown to be similar, a direct application of psychologists' generalizations should be viewed with suspicion or avoided.

Investigators in other fields are often concerned with such topics as generalization in learning, aversive behavior, or social change—phenomena not necessarily unrelated to adult education, but not specifically drawn from adult education either. Because the concepts in such studies often appear somewhat related to adult education, their allure may overpower the adult educator faced with a host of unanswered questions. But these concepts, when removed from the context in which they were developed, usually provide little or no help in solving problems in adult education. Indeed, they could mislead one to offer seriously incorrect interpretations. For example, a sociological concept that explains the dynamics between two subcultures in the context of a struggle for political power may appeal to an adult educator as an explanation of the dynamics between two groups in an educational setting. Unless there is evidence that both situations share the crucial variables that make the finding of the sociologist applicable to the problem of the educator, the educator had best not adopt the material. In order to be able to specify situational variables crucial to adult education, we must first know how to demarcate adult education.

The second erroneous assumption is that concepts can stand by themselves. Frequently researchers take concepts from one context and apply them to another. But concepts do not have an existence independent of the theoretical framework in which they were developed. An example may help to clarify our argument.

To define the concept *anxiety* is to posit assumptions about people and social transactions. Ausubel (1968) defines it using the framework of cognitive psychology, while Erikson's (1950) definition relies on psychoanalytic theory. To apply either approach, one must understand the assumptions on which the concept is predicated as well as the definition offered. When one borrows a concept, one also borrows the theoretical framework in which the concept was defined.

Related to this second error is a third: that concepts can be combined. Many adult educators borrow concepts from different sources and attempt to blend them together; for example, they combine Bandura's concept of social conditioning and Piaget's cognitive development. When one seeks to combine concepts, one is also, often unknowingly, combining theoretical frameworks. Unless one is fully versed in the basic assumptions that structure the theoretical frameworks, one may be trying to combine assumptions that directly contradict one another.

The fourth erroneous assumption, probably the most serious, is that the disciplines can define adult education. By borrowing heavily from other fields of study to define and solve problems faced in adult education, we are allowing those disciplines to define adult education for us. Our end, of course, is to find solutions to our problems but, as Dewey (1964) has so clearly pointed out, one's ends cannot, in reality, be separated from one's means. Thus, in actual practice, there are serious conflicts between the means we borrow and the ends we seek. This crucial point will be repeatedly illustrated throughout this volume. Indeed, we will argue to borrow others' means without first clarifying our ends is to allow other disciplines to define adult education for us.

These considerations naturally lead us to ask how we can develop foundations for adult education. If we agree that we should not go initially to other disciplines, asking what they have to contribute, what is the alternative?

The first step is to define the field of adult education. We need to know the nature, function, methodology, setting, and audience for adult education. Once we have a clear picture of adult education, we may ask a number of more specific questions about how to improve it, how to adapt it to new needs, and the like. Having composed our questions, we have at least three alternatives in our search for answers: (1) We can conduct research designed to answer a specific question; (2) we can reflect on our experience as adult educators for some answers; or (3) we can inquire of experts whom we have reason to believe might have answers.

The third alternative is followed in this book. Our procedure is not to apply methods from other fields to adult education, but rather to explain to a set of experts the perspective and framework of adult education and ask what they can contribute. Experts in other fields of study cannot be assumed to be experts in adult education, but they may be able to give us useful information once we have set our conceptual perspective before them. In order to structure such directives, we must be able to delineate the nature of adult education. That is our first task.

Transactional Modes

Adult education occurs in a variety of settings and modes. Correspondence courses, evening and weekend classes, intensive two-week seminars, community action groups—all are forms of adult education. One way to classify these varied situations is to define three transactional modes: individual, small group, and community. *Transactional* (Dewey and Bentley, 1949) connotes the interplay among the environment, the individuals, and the patterns of behaviors in a situation. Here we use *transactional* to characterize the nature of the learner's situation: are adults working independently and individually, in groups or classes, or as members of a community?

Transactional modes should not be confused with techniques. For example, a lecture may be used in all three transactional modes. In the individual transactional mode, a television lecture may be part of the curriculum. In the group transactional mode, an instructor or an invited speaker may lecture to the group. Similarly, lectures are frequently given at community meetings, when persons representing different sides of an issue speak or when a planning group invites a speaker to address the committee.

The individual transactional mode refers to a situation in which an adult learns by himself, for example, through participation in an independent study course. The adult does not interact with other adult learners and, more than likely, will not have face-to-face contact with the adult educator. The transaction between learner and educator takes place in their exchanges of instructional resources that further the individual's knowledge and understanding.

Many examples of individual inquiry are provided by the mass media. A person who watches a series of educational television programs, a farmer who reads an extension agent's weekly column in the local newspaper, a homemaker who listens to the homemakers' program on the radio—all are examples of the individual transactional mode. Thousands of people may be watching, reading, or listening at the same time.

In independent study, or tutorial, a teacher and a learner are paired. The learner generally spends the majority of his time as an independent learner. The tutor serves mainly as a resource person and an examiner who tests the learner's progress. A pair of learners who have no formal relationship to any educational group is an essentially similar situation. Their roles are not formally defined, but they exchange roles as their individual needs and competencies dictate.

The group transactional mode describes learning situations in which persons meet together, such as in an adult education class, to work on some problem or concern they have. Examples of this mode include classes, workshops, seminars, and short courses. The members of the group interact and may assist one another in learning. In addition to a common purpose or goal, all members of the group usually share a commitment to attend regular meetings, at specified times and places, for a set period of time; group membership remains relatively constant.

Earlier we described a learner and a teacher forming a dyad in the individual mode. Dyads may be used as an instructional technique within the group mode as well. The goals of such pairing, however, are different. While the dyad in independent study is formed to assist one learner, a dyad in the group mode (consisting of two learners) has the added and crucial task of furthering the work of the group.

When a group of citizens gathers together to resolve a problem their community faces, they are working in the community transactional mode. There are some similarities between the community mode of inquiry and the group mode. Both meet in groups. Both are concerned about exchanges among members of the group. Both may be concerned that members in the group learn. But the community group has as its primary concern problems in the community of which it is a part. Persons who participate in a community group are vitally concerned about problems created by individuals or institutions outside the group. The community problem-solving group is both influenced by and attempts to influence persons outside of the group itself. The community group has direct lines of communication to others outside the group; they feel committed and responsible to fellow citizens. Transactions in the community mode are primarily intergroup, while transactions in the group mode are solely intragroup. This is the basic difference between the two modes.

Client Focus

The transactional mode is one dimension of adult education. We shall now consider a second dimension, which we have named the *client focus*. Adult education serves three potential clients: individuals, groups, and communities. In discussing an adult education program's client focus, we are ascertaining who will primarily benefit from the educational activity—the individual, the group, or the community. Several illustrations will serve to distinguish these client focuses and show how they may be served by the transactional modes.

Consider a woman who enrolls in an adult education class to learn dressmaking. The transactional mode is group, and the client focus is individual. Then consider a class designed to help a group of administrative colleagues to work more humanely and effectively as a group. Although this educational experience will affect the individuals in the group, the group itself is the focus of the educational objective.

As a final example, consider a woman who enrolls in a correspondence course to learn about political processes. Initially, we may think she is trying to increase her individual comprehension of this content. On closer examination, however, we may find she elected correspondence study because this was the best educational mode open to her, but that she is part of a community group of individuals learning about political processes because problems in the community have become serious. Although the transactional mode is individual, the client focus is not the learner herself, but the community.

Each of the transactional modes may be used to serve each of the clientele groups. Using the general subject matter of alcoholism, we can describe the nine pairings of transactional mode and client focus.

In the individual transactional mode: (1) Individual Client Focus. An individual interested in the problems associated with alcoholism enrolls in an independent study course that outlines the characteristics of the disease and various preventive measures. The individual enrolls with the purpose of understanding the causes of alcoholism. (2) Group Client Focus. An individual who is a member of an Alcoholics Anonymous (AA) group participates in a self-organized learning program with the intent of learning how to help his AA group improve its internal dynamics. He reads books on group dynamics, talks to individuals who are members of other AA groups, and consults specialists in group dynamics. (3) Community Client Focus. An individual enrolls in an independent study course to learn about alcoholism with the intent of helping his community better understand alcoholism.

Using the same problem area, alcoholism, we can look at how the group transactional mode can serve each of the client focuses. (1) Individual Client Focus. A group of parents meets together to study problems of teenage alcoholism. All the parents in the group have teenage children with drinking problems, and they want to, in some way, help their sons and daughters. (2) Group

Client Focus. An AA group meets to improve their group's internal dynamics, interpersonal communications, and leadership dependency. (3) Community Client Focus. Citizens from various communities meet to learn how to deal with various problems of alcoholism in their home communities.

Finally, let us look at the community transactional mode: (1) Individual Client Focus. A group of citizens in a community meets to discuss what types of programs their community could offer individuals who have drinking problems. They discuss individual counseling programs for alcoholics and members of their families. (2) Group Client Focus. A community group meets to discuss how to organize an AA group in their community. Their concern is to establish a group, although individuals will, of course, benefit from the establishment of an AA group. (3) Community Client Focus. A group of local citizens meets to plan programs to help all citizens become aware of the nature of alcoholism and the extent of the problem in their community. Their focus is the entire community. Typical of such educational programs are television spots, pamphlets circulated in public libraries, and speakers at PTA meetings.

Personal, Social, and Cultural Systems

All human enterprises participate in three systems: personal, social, and cultural. These systems, as we shall now define them, constitute the third dimension of our model of adult education.

The personal system is defined by the set of distinguishing qualities or characteristics of an individual that affect his activity in a dynamic enterprise. For example, the aims a person projects are influenced by his history, abilities, and character. The personal system includes, for our purposes, such components as individuals' developmental levels, their motivation, their learning patterns, and so on.

Social systems are created each time a group of individuals forms for collective activity; each group's social system is a unique configuration. The social system includes the members' patterns of interrelating roles, the status individuals hold, the group's norms and expectations, and other similar variables. Clearly, the rules and form of a group's social system reflect its purposes and membership. While the traits and patterns of the personal and cultural systems remain fairly constant in various settings, the contours of a social system are unique to one setting.

The cultural system is structured upon the sets of beliefs, values, rules, principles, and customs that guide, in a general and pervasive manner, the conduct of persons. It includes shared assumptions about the conduct of human behavior and, as such, ethical, moral, and esthetic valuations.

The significance of each system in a given educational transaction depends on the nature of the transaction. For example, consider a sensitivity group (group transactional mode) in which members of the group are learning to develop their individual abilities (individual client focus). Here, the personal system is of paramount concern, and the social and cultural systems, while present, are not central.

Then, consider another example in the same matrix (individual as client and group transactional mode). A legislator takes a class in political science because he wants to improve his performance as a legislator. Although the class may affect his personal qualities, his primary goal is to learn to function more effectively in a particular social system, to better understand the implicit structure of that system. As in the previous example, the cultural system is of smaller significance than the personal and social. In any given educational transaction, one system may play a more significant role than the other two.

A Three-Dimensional Model

Our model for adult education now has three dimensions—transactional mode, client focus, and system—each of which has three aspects. By visualizing a cube—each plane of which represents one of our educational dimensions, one may locate a given program in terms of three coordinates: its transactional mode, client focus, and predominant system.

Using this model, we may now consider the goals of educational activities. The paramount goal of educational enterprises is growth: the growth of an individual, a group, or a community. This position has been argued by other educators and most eloquently by Dewey (1938). More extensive discussions on the meaning of growth and supporting arguments for this position will be offered by other contributors to this volume, notably Wilson (Chapter Six) and Coggins (Chapter Eleven). In brief, growth is the progressive movement towards the solution of problems and the development of abilities to encounter similar future problems with greater competencies. As mentioned earlier, educational endeavors focus on one of three potential clients; that is, they have as their central goal the growth of the individual, the group, or the community. Although a program has one client focus, one or both of the other clients, of course, may also benefit from the educational activity.

Piaget (1960) defines *growth* as adaptation, that is, the processes of assimilation and accommodation. Individuals grow as their responses, behavior, and activity become better adapted to their world. Sometimes, however, an individual develops maladaptive responses; this process is called *regression*. In considering the results of behavioral transactions, we can place them on a continuum of adaptive-maladaptive behavior. At the positive end of the continuum, progression describes individuals, groups, and communities who are in the process of realizing their potentials, that are becoming more adaptive. As they adapt, they become open to new experiences, do not feel dependent on others but interdependent, feel confident in their ability to solve problems, have a strong sense of identity, and accept responsibility. At the negative end of the continuum, maladaptive responses or regression describes behavior that results in a learner's becoming less capable of coping with problem situations than he was before he participated in the learning experience.

Applying the Model

The proposed three-dimensional model for adult education is the basis for the identification of questions that serve as organizing themes for this book. Working from this model, the contributors speak to adult education's potential for encouraging growth and even its potential for causing regression. Let us illustrate how our model may be applied to formulate questions.

First, consider the cell in the model defined by the individual transactional mode, the individual client focus, and the cultural system. A general question relevant to this cell is, What beliefs about independent study promote growth? More specific questions include the following: What cultural norms held by junior colleges about computer learning programs promote or hinder personal growth? What values adopted by educational television stations help home learners? How do the symbolic systems of educational institutions help or hinder personal growth of correspondence students?

Let us consider a second example. We select the cell of the model defined by the group transactional mode, individual client focus, and social system. A general question about this cell is, What social forces (social system) operate in small groups (group instructional mode) to help or hinder the individual in learning (individual client focus)? This broad question leads us to a series of more specific questions: What leadership roles help to promote growth in learners as members of a small class? Do different roles taken by various people in a class enhance the growth of individual members? Under what conditions is this the case? Under what conditions is this not the case?

As a final example, consider the cell identified with the group transactional mode, community client focus, and the personal system. A basic question is: What personal qualities help or hinder a small group that is working to solve community problems? The question focuses on personal qualities (the personal system), in a small group (group transactional mode) that has a community client focus.

Thus in every question related to adult education, these three dimensions—transactional modes, client focus, and systems —are clearly present. The model directs our attention to basic dimensions of adult education and, at the same time, offers us a framework in which to evaluate research and theory from various disciplines. The model allows us to view the field of adult education as central to our inquiry, rather than subsidiary to such disciplines as psychology or sociology.

The Individual
Transactional Mode

The two chapters in Part One discuss the individual transactional mode. Although Moore (Chapter Two) and Tough (Chapter Three) each make unique and fundamental contributions to our understanding of individual and self-directed learning, they address several common issues. Both, for example, stress the autonomous nature of independent learning. They would have us be more suspicious of adult educators who overstructure the adult learner's projects.

Moore provides a careful and thorough analysis of the domain of independent study. His conceptualization provides a framework through which to view the various forms of independent study. Tough makes an indisputable case for the value and central position of self-directed learning in adult education. He

Robert D. Boyd, Jerold W. ⌐

This mode⌐
education.

First, this mod⌐
structure of the natur⌐
field of adult education, ⌐
plines for its concepts, has ⌐
tion that describes the fie⌐
developed without any clear ⌐
should accomplish.

Second, our model provid⌐
and organizing problems in adult e⌐
can systematically identify problems a⌐
tionships among them.

Third, this model is based on the ⌐
tion, not on disciplines such as philosophy,
ogy. It provides a framework within which
applicability of theories and concepts developed⌐

Fourth, the model integrates instruction⌐
Traditional views of education have often divided⌐
tent, and have done violence to both in the proces⌐
considers both as intertwined in educational trans⌐
look not on instruction, not on curriculum, but on e⌐
transactions.

Fifth, our model incorporates social and cultural valu⌐
tems. Although a given program may focus on the growth o⌐
individual adult student, administrators and instructors shou⌐
not, indeed cannot, ignore cultural and social systems. Our mode⌐
provides a structure by which we may examine systematically these
various components of educational plans and programs.

This model thus corrects several serious errors among the
many that educators have labored under. It helps us specify the
nature of our enterprise and it enables us to consider systematically
the critical components of that enterprise.

correctly criticizes our failure to see the extent of adult self-directed learning. We should not, however, accept the idea that one instructional mode is of more significance than the other two; each has its values and uses. One of our major tasks in adult education is to determine the value of the different transactional modes for the three types of clients in various situations.

Both Moore and Tough discuss how some adult education programs do not pay sufficient respect to the adult learner's purposes, autonomy, and integrity. Both stress the need for adult educators to help adult learners develop the competency to learn independently. Their discussions are valuable in that educators' attitudes toward the autonomy and freedom of learners structure the ways they carry on research and practice in adult education. Certain issues have not been addressed in these chapters. One such issue is that self-directed learning is almost exclusively a middle-class phenomenon. Adult educators will be challenged, quite properly, to specify what we are doing or can do to help other classes of people make fuller use of self-directed learning. We may sidestep the challenge by claiming that such problems are basically economic or political ones, or could pass the problem on to the public schools. These would be irresponsible reactions.

Chapter Two

◆◆◆◆◆◆◆◆◆◆◆◆◆◆◆◆◆◆◆◆◆◆◆◆◆◆◆◆
◆◆◆◆◆◆◆◆◆◆◆◆◆◆◆◆◆◆◆◆◆◆◆◆◆◆

Independent Study

◆◆◆◆◆◆◆◆◆◆◆◆◆◆◆◆◆◆◆◆◆◆◆◆◆◆◆◆
◆◆◆◆◆◆◆◆◆◆◆◆◆◆◆◆◆◆◆◆◆◆◆◆◆◆

Michael G. Moore

Boyd and Apps have provided us, in Chapter One, with a model to be used in defining and describing the field of adult education and in identifying the fundamental issues of concern in the field. In this chapter, we describe the area of adult education that is usually called *independent study,* and we shall use the model to identify a number of issues that particularly concern practitioners in that field.

The use of the word *independent* to describe a large category of educational transactions leads us naturally to ask, Independent of what? As we will see, the practitioner in independent study might respond with either of two emphases, stressing the independence of the learner in time and space from the instructor, or stressing the value placed on the student's independence in making decisions that pertain to his relationship with the instructor. However, all educators will agree that all forms of independent study operate in the individual mode: When the student is actually engaged in learning, he is separated both from his teacher and from other students. Educators also agree that the indepedent student is not independent of instruction. The independent student is a person engaged in an educational program, which is to say, he is following his own deliberate strategy for changing his knowledge or behavior, and his strategy includes the use of resources that have been prepared to assist people like him. He is independent to the degree that the direction and extent of change are determined by him and the selection of resources is his.

An adult pursuing independent study is not a kind of Robinson Crusoe. He has a teacher, or many teachers, and there is a transaction between them, though the nature of the transaction is, as we shall see, different from that in the group and community modes. In this chapter, as we discuss the individual transactional mode, we use the terms *independent study* and *individual transactional mode* as synonyms. We first outline the development of the two major traditions for teaching-learning transactions in this mode. Then we characterize the relationship between learner and teacher in this mode. Finally, we use the Boyd-Apps model as a heuristic device to identify questions meriting further research.

Scholarly and Telemathic Traditions

Two distinct educational traditions inform the theory and practice of teaching and learning in the individual mode. In the scholarly tradition, the instructor monitors the student's practice of self-directed inquiry, through which the student acquires competence in study skills and the exercise of self-discipline. This form of individual student-teacher transaction, modeled on the tutorial system at the English universities of Oxford and Cambridge, was introduced to American campuses after the First World War. The tutorial model soon became known as *independent study* at Princeton, then at Stanford, and nationally after a conference sponsored by the National Research Council at the University of Iowa in 1925 (Wedemeyer, 1971).

In the scholarly tradition, independent study is a transaction between an individual student and a tutor. The student reads assigned materials, prepares papers, or engages in a project, and reports frequently to his tutor, who provides guidance and responds to the materials submitted. Independent study of this kind experienced such a growth in popularity during the 1960s that by 1973 nearly 70 percent of American colleges and universities offered such programs in all academic departments, and 90 percent offered them in at least half the departments (Dressel and Thompson, 1973). This growth in the acceptance of independent study by both instructors and learners was encouraged by the contemporaneous development of new instructional media, in particular audiovisual tapes, audio cassettes, programmed texts, and computerized teaching programs, which supplemented the older media of television, radio, and correspondence units. Instructors were able to relegate drilling practice to the audiovisual laboratory, allowing them to concentrate on diagnosing, advising, trouble shooting, and evaluating. Students discovered a new freedom in their choice of when, where, and with which media they would pursue those dimensions of study that could be explored using independent audiovisual instruction.

The second tradition in independent study is the telemathic, which means "learning at a distance." While individual tutorials in the scholarly tradition are available to only the small number of students who are enrolled in colleges and universities, the telemathic tradition has provided access to education for a large proportion of adult students over the last hundred years. According to Pyle (1965, p. 4), "the beginning of the Americanization of university extension" occurred in 1874 with Bishop John Vincent's Chautauqua movement. Educators established "home study and directed reading courses in which at one time 60,000 students were enrolled from as many as 10,000 communities."

While the separation of learner and teacher in the scholarly tradition of independent study is deliberately arranged to promote the student's self-direction and independence in working, in the telemathic tradition it is invariably a necessity imposed by the learner's social and geographical circumstances. Telemathic study is designed for adults who live too far from institutions to attend, or are unable to find classes at convenient times, or who prefer "home study." For many years, telemathic study was limited to correspondence instruction by mail. Correspondence service for independent students was inaugurated at the University of Chicago by its founder, and was introduced to the University of Wisconsin in 1906. The primary motive of these pioneers was to use the most suitable medium to facilitate the transactions between teacher and student when the latter was not able to reside on a university campus. Radio later became the medium for various experimental, and eventually successful, programs of adult education, and more recently other media have been used—television, satellite, and computer. These media are sometimes used in conjunction with traditional written correspondence, telephone conversations, or programed texts. (For descriptions of various programs, see Bannister [1969], Conger [1974], Erickson and Chausow, 1960.)

A landmark in the study of independent study is Wedemeyer's (1971) description and statement of theory, the first attempt to point out what the two traditions of independent study shared. Although this theory is still in its infancy, educators now recognize that the behaviors, attitudes, and expectations that characterize the individual mode in the scholarly tradition also exist in the telemathic tradition. Thus we are able to posit a unified philosophy and methodology for the individual mode, having some confidence that the subject of our investigation is one genus, though with many species. More important, with this understanding, we can now study the practice of each kind of independent study and test in one tradition the techniques that have been proven in the other. For example, telemathic teaching is often less structured, less directed, and more attentive to the learner's interests and concerns than collegiate independent study, while independent study on the campus makes better use of educational technology.

Transactional Distance

An essential characteristic of all independent study transactions is the physical separation of learners and teachers. Of course, there is separation between teacher and learners at some stages of any instructional program. Jackson (1971) distinguishes the preactive and the interactive stages of teaching. In the preactive phase, a teacher selects objectives and plans the curricular and instructional strategies; in the interactive phase, face-to-face with the learners, he provides verbal stimulation, makes explanations, asks questions, and provides guidance. The preactive stage of teaching occurs at a time and place apart from the learner, when the teacher is alone. In independent study, however, even the interactive phase of teaching does not require the physical presence of learners: "a teacher giving instruction over a television network is not in the physical presence of his pupils. He can even be cut off the air by a mechanical difficulty, and being unaware that anything has happened, continue to teach" (Smith, 1960, p. 235).[1]

To the best of his ability, the televised teacher performs those actions he believes necessary to help his learners. When his lesson is broadcast, his learners interact with him, making use of his verbal stimulation, his explanations, questions, and guidance. If we define a teacher by what he does, "a machine, a conventional textbook, or a programed text as well as a human being [may] be regarded as a teacher [since] one step removed from the text is the author of the text who generated the particular sequence of descriptions, explanations, interpretations, or illustrations exhibited in the text" (Henderson, 1964, p. 137).

Smith's (1960) model of teaching distinguishes among linguistic, performative, and expressive behaviors. By his verbal behavior, by example of his performance, and his nonverbal expressions, the teacher performs three kinds of instructional tasks. First, he performs a group of actions that Smith calls *logical operations*, which include defining, classifying, explaining, inferring, comparing, evaluating and designating. *Directive actions* are those that guide the students in their performance of tasks and skills. The third class of teaching behavior consists of *admonitory acts*, which include praising, reprimanding, recommending, and advising. Smith says that such verbal acts may affect psychological reinforcements or extinctions, depending upon the particular admonitory act and the circumstances in which it takes place. They are conventionally understood to be taken for their social or

◆◆◆◆◆◆◆◆◆◆◆◆◆◆◆◆◆◆◆◆◆◆◆◆◆◆◆◆◆◆◆
◆◆◆◆◆◆◆◆◆◆◆◆◆◆◆◆◆◆◆◆◆◆◆◆◆◆◆◆◆

The Individual
Transactional Mode

◆◆◆◆◆◆◆◆◆◆◆◆◆◆◆◆◆◆◆◆◆◆◆◆◆◆◆◆◆◆◆
◆◆◆◆◆◆◆◆◆◆◆◆◆◆◆◆◆◆◆◆◆◆◆◆◆◆◆◆◆

The two chapters in Part One discuss the individual transactional mode. Although Moore (Chapter Two) and Tough (Chapter Three) each make unique and fundamental contributions to our understanding of individual and self-directed learning, they address several common issues. Both, for example, stress the autonomous nature of independent learning. They would have us be more suspicious of adult educators who overstructure the adult learner's projects.

Moore provides a careful and thorough analysis of the domain of independent study. His conceptualization provides a framework through which to view the various forms of independent study. Tough makes an indisputable case for the value and central position of self-directed learning in adult education. He

Value of the Model

This model makes several contributions to the field of adult education.

First, this model contributes to demarcating a conceptual structure of the nature and parameters of adult education. The field of adult education, because it has relied heavily on other disciplines for its concepts, has suffered. Lacking an identity, a foundation that describes the field, adult education has grown and developed without any clear direction of what it is and what it should accomplish.

Second, our model provides a framework for identifying and organizing problems in adult education. Using the model, we can systematically identify problems and questions and see the relationships among them.

Third, this model is based on the structure of adult education, not on disciplines such as philosophy, psychology, or sociology. It provides a framework within which we can evaluate the applicability of theories and concepts developed in other fields.

Fourth, the model integrates instruction and curriculum. Traditional views of education have often divided form and content, and have done violence to both in the process. Our model considers both as intertwined in educational transactions. We look not on instruction, not on curriculum, but on educational transactions.

Fifth, our model incorporates social and cultural value systems. Although a given program may focus on the growth of the individual adult student, administrators and instructors should not, indeed cannot, ignore cultural and social systems. Our model provides a structure by which we may examine systematically these various components of educational plans and programs.

This model thus corrects several serious errors among the many that educators have labored under. It helps us specify the nature of our enterprise and it enables us to consider systematically the critical components of that enterprise.

correctly criticizes our failure to see the extent of adult self-directed learning. We should not, however, accept the idea that one instructional mode is of more significance than the other two; each has its values and uses. One of our major tasks in adult education is to determine the value of the different transactional modes for the three types of clients in various situations.

Both Moore and Tough discuss how some adult education programs do not pay sufficient respect to the adult learner's purposes, autonomy, and integrity. Both stress the need for adult educators to help adult learners develop the competency to learn independently. Their discussions are valuable in that educators' attitudes toward the autonomy and freedom of learners structure the ways they carry on research and practice in adult education. Certain issues have not been addressed in these chapters. One such issue is that self-directed learning is almost exclusively a middle-class phenomenon. Adult educators will be challenged, quite properly, to specify what we are doing or can do to help other classes of people make fuller use of self-directed learning. We may sidestep the challenge by claiming that such problems are basically economic or political ones, or could pass the problem on to the public schools. These would be irresponsible reactions.

Chapter Two

◆◆◆◆◆◆◆◆◆◆◆◆◆◆◆◆◆◆◆◆◆◆◆◆
◆◆◆◆◆◆◆◆◆◆◆◆◆◆◆◆◆◆◆◆◆◆◆◆

Independent Study

◆◆◆◆◆◆◆◆◆◆◆◆◆◆◆◆◆◆◆◆◆◆◆◆
◆◆◆◆◆◆◆◆◆◆◆◆◆◆◆◆◆◆◆◆◆◆◆◆

Michael G. Moore

Boyd and Apps have provided us, in Chapter One, with a model to be used in defining and describing the field of adult education and in identifying the fundamental issues of concern in the field. In this chapter, we describe the area of adult education that is usually called *independent study,* and we shall use the model to identify a number of issues that particularly concern practitioners in that field.

      The use of the word *independent* to describe a large category of educational transactions leads us naturally to ask, Independent of what? As we will see, the practitioner in independent study might respond with either of two emphases, stressing the independence of the learner in time and space from the instructor, or stressing the value placed on the student's independence in making decisions that pertain to his relationship with the instructor. However, all educators will agree that all forms of independent study operate in the individual mode: When the student is actually engaged in learning, he is separated both from his teacher and from other students. Educators also agree that the indepedent student is not independent of instruction. The independent student is a person engaged in an educational program, which is to say, he is following his own deliberate strategy for changing his knowledge or behavior, and his strategy includes the use of resources that have been prepared to assist people like him. He is independent to the degree that the direction and extent of change are determined by him and the selection of resources is his.

An adult pursuing independent study is not a kind of Robinson Crusoe. He has a teacher, or many teachers, and there is a transaction between them, though the nature of the transaction is, as we shall see, different from that in the group and community modes. In this chapter, as we discuss the individual transactional mode, we use the terms *independent study* and *individual transactional mode* as synonyms. We first outline the development of the two major traditions for teaching-learning transactions in this mode. Then we characterize the relationship between learner and teacher in this mode. Finally, we use the Boyd-Apps model as a heuristic device to identify questions meriting further research.

Scholarly and Telemathic Traditions

Two distinct educational traditions inform the theory and practice of teaching and learning in the individual mode. In the scholarly tradition, the instructor monitors the student's practice of self-directed inquiry, through which the student acquires competence in study skills and the exercise of self-discipline. This form of individual student-teacher transaction, modeled on the tutorial system at the English universities of Oxford and Cambridge, was introduced to American campuses after the First World War. The tutorial model soon became known as *independent study* at Princeton, then at Stanford, and nationally after a conference sponsored by the National Research Council at the University of Iowa in 1925 (Wedemeyer, 1971).

In the scholarly tradition, independent study is a transaction between an individual student and a tutor. The student reads assigned materials, prepares papers, or engages in a project, and reports frequently to his tutor, who provides guidance and responds to the materials submitted. Independent study of this kind experienced such a growth in popularity during the 1960s that by 1973 nearly 70 percent of American colleges and universities offered such programs in all academic departments, and 90 percent offered them in at least half the departments (Dressel and Thompson, 1973). This growth in the acceptance of independent study by both instructors and learners was encouraged by the contemporaneous development of new instructional media, in particular audiovisual tapes, audio cassettes, programmed texts, and computerized teaching programs, which supplemented the older media of television, radio, and correspondence units. Instructors were able to relegate drilling practice to the audiovisual laboratory, allowing them to concentrate on diagnosing, advising, trouble shooting, and evaluating. Students discovered a new freedom in their choice of when, where, and with which media they would pursue those dimensions of study that could be explored using independent audiovisual instruction.

The second tradition in independent study is the telemathic, which means "learning at a distance." While individual tutorials in the scholarly tradition are available to only the small number of students who are enrolled in colleges and universities, the telemathic tradition has provided access to education for a large proportion of adult students over the last hundred years. According to Pyle (1965, p. 4), "the beginning of the Americanization of university extension" occurred in 1874 with Bishop John Vincent's Chautauqua movement. Educators established "home study and directed reading courses in which at one time 60,000 students were enrolled from as many as 10,000 communities."

While the separation of learner and teacher in the scholarly tradition of independent study is deliberately arranged to promote the student's self-direction and independence in working, in the telemathic tradition it is invariably a necessity imposed by the learner's social and geographical circumstances. Telemathic study is designed for adults who live too far from institutions to attend, or are unable to find classes at convenient times, or who prefer "home study." For many years, telemathic study was limited to correspondence instruction by mail. Correspondence service for independent students was inaugurated at the University of Chicago by its founder, and was introduced to the University of Wisconsin in 1906. The primary motive of these pioneers was to use the most suitable medium to facilitate the transactions between teacher and student when the latter was not able to reside on a university campus. Radio later became the medium for various experimental, and eventually successful, programs of adult education, and more recently other media have been used—television, satellite, and computer. These media are sometimes used in conjunction with traditional written correspondence, telephone conversations, or programed texts. (For descriptions of various programs, see Bannister [1969], Conger [1974], Erickson and Chausow, 1960.)

A landmark in the study of independent study is Wedemeyer's (1971) description and statement of theory, the first attempt to point out what the two traditions of independent study shared. Although this theory is still in its infancy, educators now recognize that the behaviors, attitudes, and expectations that characterize the individual mode in the scholarly tradition also exist in the telemathic tradition. Thus we are able to posit a unified philosophy and methodology for the individual mode, having some confidence that the subject of our investigation is one genus, though with many species. More important, with this understanding, we can now study the practice of each kind of independent study and test in one tradition the techniques that have been proven in the other. For example, telemathic teaching is often less structured, less directed, and more attentive to the learner's interests and concerns than collegiate independent study, while independent study on the campus makes better use of educational technology.

Transactional Distance

An essential characteristic of all independent study transactions is the physical separation of learners and teachers. Of course, there is separation between teacher and learners at some stages of any instructional program. Jackson (1971) distinguishes the preactive and the interactive stages of teaching. In the preactive phase, a teacher selects objectives and plans the curricular and instructional strategies; in the interactive phase, face-to-face with the learners, he provides verbal stimulation, makes explanations, asks questions, and provides guidance. The preactive stage of teaching occurs at a time and place apart from the learner, when the teacher is alone. In independent study, however, even the interactive phase of teaching does not require the physical presence of learners: "a teacher giving instruction over a television network is not in the physical presence of his pupils. He can even be cut off the air by a mechanical difficulty, and being unaware that anything has happened, continue to teach" (Smith, 1960, p. 235).[1]

To the best of his ability, the televised teacher performs those actions he believes necessary to help his learners. When his lesson is broadcast, his learners interact with him, making use of his verbal stimulation, his explanations, questions, and guidance. If we define a teacher by what he does, "a machine, a conventional textbook, or a programed text as well as a human being [may] be regarded as a teacher [since] one step removed from the text is the author of the text who generated the particular sequence of descriptions, explanations, interpretations, or illustrations exhibited in the text" (Henderson, 1964, p. 137).

Smith's (1960) model of teaching distinguishes among linguistic, performative, and expressive behaviors. By his verbal behavior, by example of his performance, and his nonverbal expressions, the teacher performs three kinds of instructional tasks. First, he performs a group of actions that Smith calls *logical operations*, which include defining, classifying, explaining, inferring, comparing, evaluating and designating. *Directive actions* are those that guide the students in their performance of tasks and skills. The third class of teaching behavior consists of *admonitory acts*, which include praising, reprimanding, recommending, and advising. Smith says that such verbal acts may affect psychological reinforcements or extinctions, depending upon the particular admonitory act and the circumstances in which it takes place. They are conventionally understood to be taken for their social or emotional impact upon the pupil rather than for their cognitive content.

In independent study, teachers communicate their logical, directive, and admonitory actions to students distant in time and space. Like classroom teachers, they can communicate through words, performance, or nonverbal expression, though the extent to which they use each depends on the characteristics of the communications media they employ.

Thus, in independent study, the students' transactions with their teachers occur through the use of electronic or print media. Some educational transactions are more distant than others; this distance is not a matter of geographical location. The transactional distance is a function of two crucial variables in the learner-teacher transaction, which we have chosen to call *dialogue* and *structure*.

Dialogue describes two-way communication between student and teacher. For example, telemathic programs that encourage telephone communication allow for frequent dialogue, while those that use only radio programs make dialogue impossible. In programs in which there is a high degree of dialogue, the transactional distance is less than in programs in which little dialogue is possible.

Structure is the extent to which the objectives, implementation procedures, and evaluation procedures of a teaching program are prepared, or can be adapted, to meet specific objectives, implementation plans, and evaluation methods of individual students. Structure is a measure of the educational program's responsiveness to the learner's individual needs. Highly structured programs define the material and skills for the students and thus are transactionally distant from the individual learner. Highly structured programs such as linear, nonbranching programed texts allow no variation in the program. Correspondence programs are likely to be somewhat less structured, as the teachers respond to the individual student's questions and assignments.

The two variables of dialogue and structure may be used to generate four general types of telemathic programs:

1. Programs with no dialogue and no structure, such as television and radio courses. (This type is the most distant.)

2. Programs with no dialogue and some structure, such as self-directed independent reading programs.
3. Programs with dialogue and high structure, such as correspondence courses.
4. Programs with dialogue and no structure, such as open-ended, personal tutorials. (This type is the least distant.)

Of course, individual programs have their characteristic transactions, but these four types broadly define the variable of distance.

Programs in which the distance between teacher and learner is small, because dialogue is easy and structure is minimal, allow teacher and learner to respond easily to one another. In such programs, admonitory teaching behaviors as well as directive action and logical operations are possible. However, in programs that offer little dialogue and high structure, admonitory acts are difficult or impossible. Some programed texts, for example, attempt to establish some dialogue between teacher and learner by use of the branching technique. But the admonitory acts, such as "Ooops! You didn't follow instructions" (Mager, 1962, p. 5), are weak in contrast to the power such statements would carry in a highly dialogic interaction. Although even the most distant teachers are able to communicate logical operations, directive and admonitory actions are more easily communicated in transactions that are less distant. A particular learner's success in a distant telematic program depends on the extent to which he can work without directive and admonitory communication. This is determined by his competence as an autonomous, or self-directed, learner—the topic to which we now turn.

Autonomous Learning

Jackson's (1971) theory of preactive and interactive phases of teaching and Smith's (1960) theory of teacher behaviors assume that, in an educational transaction, teaching always precedes learning; they place most of the responsibility for decisions about the transaction with the teacher. For Jackson, behavior relevant to teaching includes preparing lesson plans, arranging furniture and equipment within the room, marking papers, studying test reports, reading sections of a textbook, and thinking about the aberrant behavior of particular students. This approach grants the teacher more decision-making power than is acceptable to many adult educators, who emphasize the desirability of having learners participate in the selection of objectives, instructional procedures, and evaluative criteria. It also suggests the learner is very dependent on the teacher for explanations, guidance, questions, and stimulation. Maslow describes teaching that posits the learner's dependence in the following terms: "the teacher is the active one, who teaches a passive person who gets shaped and taught and who is given something which he then accumulates and which he may then lose or retain, depending upon the efficiency of the initial indoctrination process. . . . This kind of learning too easily reflects the goals of the teacher and ignores the values and ends of the learner himself" (1968, p. 57).

While some adult learners need help in formulating their learning objectives, in identifying sources of information, and in measuring achievement, many other learners do not need such guidance. These are the autonomous learners. A fully autonomous learner is a person who can identify his learning need when he finds a problem to be solved, a skill to be acquired, or information to be obtained. He is able to articulate his need in the form of a general goal, differentiate that goal into several specific objectives, and define fairly explicitly his criteria for successful achievement. In implementing his need, he gathers the information he desires, collects ideas, practices skills, works to resolve his problems, and achieves his goals. In evaluating, the learner judges the appropriateness of newly acquired skills, the adequacy of his solutions, and the quality of his new ideas and knowledge. He reaches conclusions, accepting or rejecting the material, and eventually decides his goals have been achieved, or can be abandoned.

The autonomous learner is thus independent. Heathers (1955) defines two types of independence, instrumental and emotional, that characterize the autonomous learner. *Instrumental independence* comprises the abilities to act, solve problems, and persist in a given task without asking for instruction or help. *Emotional independence* consists of the ability to act without needing the reassurance, affection, or approval of others. It includes self-assertion, in the form of the need to master tasks, which is motivated by the need for self-approval of one's performance.

The autonomous learner is emotionally independent when pursuing a learning task, motivated primarily by his need for self-approval. He is also likely to have a high degree of instrumental independence, since he is experienced in coping with learning problems in a self-reliant manner, but may be instrumentally dependent at times, for he will ask for help after persistent attempts to solve a problem prove unrewarding. However, his approach to a helper is functional, not emotional; he requests help to achieve his ends, not to win the approval of the helper. An autonomous learner proceeds without need for admonition and little need for direction. If highly autonomous, he may have no personal relationship with a teacher; if he has a personal teacher, will be able to control the relationship by resisting direction and admonition that do not suit his goals. He is also able to control and manage alternative sources of help. This description is very similar to Boyd's definition of the adult learner, a person who "can approach subject matter directly without having an adult in a set of intervening roles between the learner and the subject matter. The adult knows his own standards and expectations. He no longer needs to be told, nor does he require approval and rewards from persons in authority" (1966, p. 180).

According to Knowles, autonomous behavior should be natural for the adult learner who, by definition, conceives of himself as self-directed: "the point at which a person becomes an adult, psychologically, is that point at which he perceives himself to be wholly self-directing" (1970, pp. 42–43). Knowles views dependency as part of the self-concept of a child. As one grows older, one sees oneself as having the capacity to make decisions and one's self-identity begins to assume a form. Unfortunately, in elementary and secondary schools, the student finds that the responsibility for his learning is borne by his teachers, school administrators, and his parents. Some students respond to this by conceiving of themselves as passive and dependent in all educational transactions. For this reason, adult educators often must help learners to overcome a fear of being self-directed and self-reliant in learning, for adults are typically not prepared for self-directed learning; they need to develop an independent stance in educational transactions.

A number of observers have criticized the schools for foster-
ing dependency and neglecting the learner's autonomy. Thelen
says that schools, by keeping students busy finding solutions to
problems that are "externalized, depersonalized, and emotionally
fumigated," deny their students "the most fundamental human
need: the quest for autonomy" (1972, p. 27). According to Rogers,
the vast majority of schools at all levels of education "are locked
into a traditional and conventional approach which makes significant learning improbable if not impossible. When we put together
in one scheme such elements as a prescribed curriculum, similar
assignments for all students, lecturing as almost the only mode of
instruction, standard tests by which all students are externally
evaluated and instructor chosen grades as the measure of learning,
then we can almost guarantee that meaningful learning will be at
an absolute minimum" (1969, p. 5).

Yet autonomy is the stated objective of most educators. Most
would agree with Bruner that "instruction is the provisional state
that has as its object to make the learner or problem solver self-
sufficient" (1966, p. 53) and with Bryson that "self-education is the
goal of all adult education" (1948, p. 31). And most would agree
with Rogers that learners need to learn "how to learn . . . how to
adapt and change" and to realize "that no knowledge is secure, that
only the process of seeking knowledge gives a basis for security"
(1969, p. 104).

Since autonomy is presumed to be descriptive of adult behavior, the critical task for adult educators is to restore and support
the learner's autonomy. Knowles (1970) argues that programs in
adult education must show adult learners how to diagnose their
learning needs, plan their learning programs, and evaluate their
progress. In adult education, learners and teachers must share
responsibility for their educational transactions. Implicit in this
consideration of the adult learner's autonomy is a respect for his
integrity as a person. Boyd (1969, p. 186) reminds us that "an
individual has the right and responsibility to determine, in concert
with those directly involved, the direction and extent of his acts in
accordance with the knowledge of the realities and his capabilities
to handle the demands of those realities."

Another reason for involving the adult learner in all stages
of his learning program is efficiency. Adults, unlike children, "en-

gage in learning largely in response to pressures they feel from their current life situation" (Knowles, 1970, p. 50). They learn not so much for their future as for their problems in the present, and if the objectives of an educational program are relevant to such problems, the learner's motivation is high. Thus the question of how to motivate adult learners, a problem that preoccupies many teachers, becomes irrelevant. The art of teaching the autonomous learner consists of helping him decide what is a suitable objective for his natural wish to learn, and then helping him pursue that objective. Rogers writes, "I become very irritated with the notion that students must be 'motivated'. The young human being is intrinsically motivated at a high degree. Many elements of his environment constitute challenges for him. He is curious, eager to discover, eager to know, eager to solve problems . . . it is our task as facilitators of learning to tap that motivation, to discover what challenges are real for the young person, and to provide the opportunity for him to meet those challenges" (1969, p. 131).

Thus adult learners must be treated by educators as autonomous learners who exercise their autonomy at all stages of the program. After helping a learner identify his objectives, the educator aids him to discover the appropriate resources, define relevant goals, and specify evaluative criteria. At each stage, the educator helps the learner to be as active in the educational transaction as he is able.

As adult learners vary in their ability to learn autonomously, independent study courses vary in the extent to which they encourage learners to exercise autonomy. In the most autonomous programs, the learner is responsible for selecting his objectives, his program of study (including choice of resources, sequence, and pace), and the criteria and method for evaluation. In the least autonomous courses, all the decisions are made for the learner by the instructor. Between these two extremes fall a wide range of programs that permit autonomy in some areas and not others.

Independent Study and the Boyd-Apps Model

The image that the reader should now have of the individualized mode in adult education is one of numerous institutions delivering, through various media, any of a vast range of instructional programs in response to the demands of learners who are more or less autonomous in deciding what, when, where, and how they will learn. Within the institutions, professional educators and supporting ancillary workers plan and implement programs in anticipation of the demands of learners. We conclude our discussion by returning to the Boyd-Apps model, using the model to elicit representative questions for research and discussion.

Client Focus. Most independent study programs have an individual client focus, though the proportion of programs with a group or community focus offered by a particular institution depends upon the mission of the institution. Certainly the individual is the focus of most offerings by university extension independent study departments, which teach undergraduate courses to distant students. Similarly, all high school correspondence courses, many educational radio and television programs, and other academic courses are focused on the individual client.

Most telemathic institutions also sponsor noncredit, nonacademic programs, which also have an individual client focus. Subjects for such independent courses include consumer education, etiquette, child care, and carpet installation. Noncredit programs with an individual focus are also provided by radio and television stations, and by adult basic education programs such as the Rural Family Development program in Wisconsin, whose goal is to improve the living skills of rural families through teaching by television, radio, and telephone. Similar programs can be found in every country in the world (Conger, 1974).

The individual focus also dominates many independent study programs in professional development for persons in various professions. Institutions offer these programs, through various media, for medical personnel, school counselors and teachers, librarians, business managers, and others. These programs differ from most of those mentioned earlier in that, because the learner is a professional who will use the knowledge or skills gained in the course to help his own clients, the courses have an indirect community focus.

Independent study courses that have a primary focus on the community are available, though certainly less common than programs with an individual focus. The most common are designed for students in the helping professions who work in fields of community development. Independent study programs with a similar focus are especially valuable in the national development programs of countries that have few teachers. In Kenya, for example, an important program with a community focus is a radio and correspondence course that provides in-service training for a large portion of the country's school teachers.

At the University of Illinois, the PLATO program includes some very interesting examples of computer assisted educational programs with a community focus. "Alternative Futures" allows learners to explore how possible technological and social developments will affect our future. In "Boneyard Creek," the computer facilitates the exchange of different viewpoints on solving an environmental problem, and in "Future of the University" the computer acts as a mediator among groups arguing about future developments at the university. Lastly, agencies such as the United States Postal Service and the Health Insurance Association of America administer programs designed to meet the learning needs of employees who wish to improve their skills and increase their knowledge. Such employer sponsored programs aid employees to increase their contribution to the organizational community.

System. The cultural system appears to dominate the behavior of those who design and teach in independent study. This emphasis is not surprising in that individual growth is in part a function of knowledge about cultural areas—including foreign languages, history, mathematics, technology, and so forth—and a function of increased competence in culturally bound skills such as reading.

Cultural knowledge lends itself to independent study, but there is a danger that in structuring such studies, adult educators may neglect to give attention to an important problem that is comprised in the personal system. The educator must consider the degree of autonomy that a particular learner is able to exercise. The instructor needs to structure his materials and conduct his dialogue in ways that will permit learners to become more autonomous during the course of the program. This personal growth must be a primary educational goal regardless of the course's subject matter. But, a learner cannot learn effectively if the educational transaction demands more autonomy than he is able to exercise. Thus, the teacher must structure the materials for learners who are absent in space and time, and who have varied competencies as autonomous learners.

Another set of problems in the personal system concerns the curriculum. In some independent study programs—for example, those that have little dialogue—little or no personal relationships between teacher and student exists. A consequent problem for teachers and for learners in independent study is to identify correctly what learning and teaching objectives are likely to require substantial personal interaction, thus making them unsuitable goals for telemathic methods. Such goals the autonomous student must address in face-to-face group settings.

Finally, we can identify in the personal system a set of questions about the predictability of success in the use of independent study. For example, are particular personality characteristics predictive of achievement in this transactional mode? Blitz and Smith (1973) ascertained that success in computer assisted instruction can be predicted from personality characteristics measured by the Edwards Personal Preference Schedule. Baskin and Keeton (1962) found that students in independent study on campus were high in need achievement, and there is some evidence that distance students are high in field independence, but other cognitive styles have not yet been researched.[2]

Although independent students do not actually meet with their teachers, we can identify some questions of a social nature that require attention. Although they are separate, perhaps never having met, students and teachers in independent study are confronted with the issues of role and authority. In practice, in those programs that have substantial dialogue, both teachers and learners tend to introduce to their relationship expectations about roles and authority that they derived from other educational experiences. The consequent problems can be as great for the conservative student faced with a liberal instructor as for a teacher from a conventional, authoritarian academic background in correspondence with a highly autonomous and self-willed student. Both teachers and students need to learn to appreciate the essentially nonauthoritarian, responsive role of the telemathic teacher and the ultimate authority of the adult learner. In particular, the less than fully autonomous student needs to learn to adopt an aggressive consumerist approach to his teaching resources.[3]

Toward the Future

The theory and practice of independent study described in this chapter are founded on a set of values and assumptions about human behavior. The values are those of Western culture, notably individualism, freedom from unreasonable controls, democratic participation, personal authority and responsibility, and freedom of choice. Because independent study emphasizes the learner's autonomy, these values are asserted more often than before in the field of educational practice, and especially in higher education, where institutions have sometimes been authoritarian rather than democratic. Various practical questions will have to be addressed by educators, institutions, and students. How, in practice, can a learner design his own curriculum? How can the professional give guidance without being coercive? To what extent can the learner be an originator and source of knowledge? How will the new practices of telemathic instruction affect higher education? How will a new generation of school teachers accustomed to independent study affect elementary and secondary schooling?

We should also consider the effects in industry, in leisure, and, perhaps most important, in political life of a growing population that is experienced and confident in setting and meeting learning objectives with no particular regard for authority. For example, will such individuals have an effect on local government? At the international level, can foreign cultures borrow telematic teaching technology without accepting also the values of autonomous learning? Might technology then be used to reduce freedom rather than increase it?

These are questions in the cultural system, and they are more difficult to research than those that arise in the personal or social systems. Perhaps they can only be proposed for consideration as we proceed to rebuild old institutions and design new ones.

New and changed institutions will certainly be a consequence of the growing confidence with which the values of independent study are now asserted. As large numbers of people study in courses that are open to change by learners, the numbers able to learn, act, and think autonomously will increase.

Adult learning need no longer be random, for through independent study, self-directed adults can expect to be served by professional resources in planning and implementing their learning. This is surely a significant move towards a system of lifelong education and towards the reality of a learning society.

Comments by the Senior Authors

[1] Some readers may find Smith's position difficult to accept, because they would argue that teaching does not occur unless a student is learning. The issue is whether we define teaching as an intention or as an event. Smith accepts the definition of teaching as the instructor's intention.

[2] In Chapter Six, Wilson provides the reader with a concise introduction to cognitive styles, of which field independence is one. Wilson's material nicely complements Moore's discussion.

[3] Moore's observation on the relationships between learners and teachers may be compared with Robinson's in Chapter Five. Robinson reviews a set of variables that affect the individual in a learning situation. Although Robinson discusses the group transactional mode, his material is relevant to Moore's discussion.

Chapter Three

◆◆◆◆◆◆◆◆◆◆◆◆◆◆◆◆◆◆◆◆◆◆◆◆◆◆
◆◆◆◆◆◆◆◆◆◆◆◆◆◆◆◆◆◆◆◆◆◆◆◆◆◆

Individual Learning

◆◆◆◆◆◆◆◆◆◆◆◆◆◆◆◆◆◆◆◆◆◆◆◆◆◆
◆◆◆◆◆◆◆◆◆◆◆◆◆◆◆◆◆◆◆◆◆◆◆◆◆◆

Allen Tough

Both practitioners and researchers in adult education have recently shown a sudden surge of interest in the individual transactional mode. Adult educators are finding individual adult learning to be of major significance. In this chapter, we first distinguish three forms of individual learning and note the relative frequency of each. We then discuss the reasons for choosing the individual learning mode, examine the client focus, and offer some suggestions for the adult educator interested in individual learning. We conclude by presenting three future frontiers in theory and research and summarizing the present status of our knowledge about individual learning.

Forms of Learning in the Individual Mode

For many years, adult educators have been familiar with the flexibility and other benefits of correspondence courses, independent study courses, and home study. Universities, proprietary schools, and the armed forces have been leaders in providing these courses. The designer of such a course develops a series of lessons that includes reading materials, exercises, and perhaps tests that monitor a student's progress. Each lesson is provided as a convenient package, and the exercises or tests are marked by someone at the central educational institution.

More recently, adult educators have been experimenting with television programs, language tapes and records, videotapes, and programed textbooks. Today, virtually no one doubts the usefulness of such learning methods, at least for certain learners and certain subjects. The learner can benefit from having a highly skilled professional plan a detailed series of learning steps for him to follow.

How common are correspondence study, programed and individualized instruction materials, and other methods just listed? In early studies reported by Tough (1971) of a variety of populations in Toronto, Canada, 3 percent of adult learning projects fell into this category. A *learning project* was defined as a highly deliberate effort to gain and retain certain definite knowledge and skill through a series of related learning sessions that last at least seven hours. Several subsequent studies of various populations throughout the United States and in four other countries tend to confirm this figure, though the proportion has ranged as low as 1 percent for professional men (McCatty, 1973) and as high as 19 percent for Atlanta pharmacists (Johns, 1973).

A second type of learning within the individual mode is that in which an instructor, or other expert, facilitates the learning, working with a single student. This is the way many of us learn to drive a car, to play the piano, or to play tennis. Such individual lessons constitute about 10 percent of all adult learning projects. Reported frequencies range from 6 percent among a group of managers and teachers in West Africa (Denys, 1973) to 14 percent among a group of adults working toward high school completion in Florida (Johnson, 1973). Some adult educators, proprietary schools, and self-employed instructors have paid attention to this learning situation, but virtually no researchers have yet studied it in depth.

Self-planned learning, which constitutes about 73 percent of all highly deliberate adult learning, is a third type of learning situation within the individual transactional mode. Self-planned learning is quite different from the previous two types, in which an expert or professional person plans a sequence of learning activities for the learner and also provides most of the subject matter and materials. In self-planned learning, the learner retains the primary responsibility for the detailed day-to-day decisions about what and how to learn during each learning session. In addition, the learner uses a variety of sources for the subject matter—largely books and people—and locates these resources himself.[1]

Almost any knowledge and skill can be included in the wide range of subject matter that is learned through self-planned programs. Many self-planned efforts are related to the learner's job: the study of new processes and methods, the gathering of information needed for making decisions or preparing for new responsibilities, and the investigations pursued by organizational committees. Other self-planned learning is related to home and family: child-rearing, repairing the wiring on the car, gathering information and opinions before a major purchase, gardening, sewing, health, cooking, and studying interpersonal relationships in the family or principles and practices of women's and men's liberation. In addition, people learn on their own to play a new sport, game, or musical instrument. And much self-planned learning delves into history, current events, psychic phenomena, literature, politics, science, psychology, religion, and other subjects that satisfy our curiosity and broaden our horizons.

An example of a self-planned effort to learn is a program devised by a woman who wanted to learn to speak Spanish. She devoted seventeen sessions, spread over several weeks, to memorizing and practicing her Spanish vocabulary, using a list of five hundred basic words that she found in a book. Between these vocabulary sessions, she conversed with a bilingual acquaintance, listened occasionally to a Spanish radio station, read about Spanish grammar and usage in an introductory textbook, and attended a meeting conducted in Spanish. Clearly the learner herself retained the overall responsibility for planning the sequence of her learning activities and selecting various resources, including people and media, for the subject matter.

Until a few years ago, all of us focused our attention exclusively on the highly visible and salient forms of adult learning, such as evening classes. Coolican (1974) reports, however that learning mediated through a class, a workshop, or some other group with or without an instructor accounts for only about 14 percent of adults' total range of major learning efforts, while self-planned learning accounts for about 73 percent. Table 1, based on all studies to date, provides a more detailed summary.

As more adult educators think about the implications of this fresh picture of adult learning, both practice and theory in the field may change greatly. Administrators of schools, colleges, libraries, museums, and educational departments of the media may wish to redesign their programs to reflect the actual pattern of adult education. (Major implications for practice are included in Hiemstra's 1975b, study of older adults; studies of teachers by Fair, 1973, and Kelley, 1976; and surveys by Peters and Gordon, 1974, and Penland, 1977.)

Table 1. Learning Efforts in the Individual Mode

The Major Planner of the Learning Sessions	Percentage of Efforts Planned by a Professional[a]	Percentage of Efforts Planned by an Amateur or Peer
A group or its leader-instructor	10	4[b]
One person in a one-to-one interaction	7	3
Preprogramed media and resources[c]	3	0
The learner	0	73
Total	20	80

Note: Data in this table are based on twenty-one studies of major learning efforts or learning projects. The general finding is that the typical person conducts five distinct learning projects in one year and spends an average of 100 hours on each learning project.

[a] *Professional* refers to anyone who is trained, paid, or institutionally designated to facilitate the learning. Friends and peers are here considered to be amateurs at planning.

[b] Excellent studies of these autonomous learning groups are provided by Knoepfli (1971) and Farquharson (1973).

[c] Examples are programed instruction, television, radio, correspondence courses, phonograph records, and tapes.

Why Choose the Individual Mode?

Over the years, several educators have discussed various learning efforts that are somewhat similar, but not identical, to individual learning projects. They have labeled their activities *self-education, self-instruction, self-teaching, individual learning, independent study, self-directed learning,* and *self-study.* Individuals engaged in such efforts to learn have been called *autonomous learners, self-propelled learners, self-teachers,* and *autodidacts.* Individual adult learning has been common and important throughout the world and throughout history, as Grattan (1955) and Houle (1961) have noted.

Why is individual learning so popular among adults? Why do adults so often choose to handle the detailed planning themselves, rather than turn to someone else? Why do adult learners so often choose and obtain a variety of learning resources (individuals, groups, books, and television) instead of simply turning the instructional task over to one group or teacher?

McCatty (1973) provides some specific responses to these questions. He asked his interviewees their reasons for choosing to learn certain things individually instead of in a group. The most common reason was the desire for individualized subject matter. Several of the interviewees had such specific problems or interests that they believed that available courses were too general to be suitable. A second common reason for choosing to learn individually was the convenience of learning at home. Other learners cited a certain facet of their personality as their reason. One interviewee said that he had to prove to himself that he could do things. Others mentioned the desire for independence and self-reliance.

One might ask how people get started in self-planned learning. My hunch is that this is such a natural way of learning that it is common from a very early age. Perhaps we should ask quite a different question: Why, from the age of five, do we push children so often into learning in a group? Learning on one's own seems so much more natural.[2]

One might also ask what benefits adults expect to gain from their individual learning efforts? There are many other ways a person could spend the same amount of time, some of which would provide more pleasure or income than the learning efforts. Why then does the adult spend time learning?

In most adult learning efforts, the learner does not simply want to possess certain knowledge or skills, he wants to apply them to a particular project or problem. We can depict this motivation as a three-step sequence of expected benefits. In the first step, the learner engages in certain learning activities because he assumes that these activities will lead him to acquire and retain certain knowledge and skill. In the second step, then, the learner is always the beneficiary as he now possesses the new knowledge and skill. But in adult education there is usually a third step: The learner assumes that this new knowledge and skill will make it possible for him to better perform some task.

Using several examples from Chapter One, we can illustrate the three steps. An adult studies alcoholism, the disease and its prevention (step one). He acquires and retains certain knowledge about alcoholism (step two) and uses it to assess and arrest his own drinking problem (step three). Similarly, an adult reads and asks about group dynamics; he acquires and retains certain knowledge and skills; he uses these to help his Alcoholics Anonymous group function better. Or, an adult takes correspondence lessons on the political process; he acquires and retains certain knowledge and skills; he uses these to facilitate his community's political process.

As we turn our attention to the learner's anticipated use of the knowledge and skill, focuses other than the individual client are evident. The knowledge and skill are used primarily for the learner's own benefit in the first example, largely for a group's benefit in the second example, and for the benefit of the community in the third.

The concept of client focus provided in Chapter One is thought-provoking and therefore useful. But, in my opinion, Boyd and Apps have placed too strong an emphasis on the importance of the client focus. I have two reasons for saying this. First, from interviews I have conducted, I have found that the adult learner's expected uses of knowledge and skill are quite varied and complex, even in a single learning project. By dividing these uses neatly into three categories, the model greatly oversimplifies the picture, and omits several important dimensions. Second, the client focus would seem to make very little difference to the format and process of the learning transaction in actual practice.

One other problem results from using the Boyd-Apps model. In the dimension of transactional mode, the word *individual* refers to the learner. But the term *individual client focus* refers to either the learner or some other individual as the beneficiary. For example, a learner may be studying primarily to help a relative (to help him treat his alcoholism) or employer (to meet new problems at work). The model would be more useful if it distinguished between learner client focus and other individual client focus.[3]

Some Fundamental Questions

Several issues are raised in various sections of this chapter, but some particularly significant issues come to mind at this stage.

First, is the majority of individual learning worthy of attention? For example, is it important to the individual or to society? Is the amount of knowledge and skill learned in this mode substantial? Are learners enthusiastic about what they learn in this mode? Tough (1971) reports that learners rate their individual learning higher than their group learning in terms of their accomplishment and enthusiasm. Larger, precise studies could provide more convincing information.

Second, Boyd and Apps raised several important issues about the limitations of self-planned learning in their responses to the second draft of this chapter. They asked: "Which areas are acceptable for self-study? Are there areas in which one does not appropriately engage in self-study? The most vivid example that we can think of is a course in medicine. Does society resist or reject the idea that self-study can lead to professional preparation?"

My response is simple: far fewer areas are inappropriate for self-planned learning than one might at first think. Practicing doctors, of course, engage in more self-planned learning than most people we have interviewed. They devote an enormous amount of time to learning in order to keep up with their field and to treat particular cases (McCatty, 1973). Self-planned learning has also been conducted for several years with remarkable success in at least one medical school: McMaster University in Hamilton, Ontario,

Canada. Students learn largely on their own or in teams that focus on particular cases and problems, instead of attending lectures and classes. Students preparing for almost any occupation could do some learning on their own. Educational institutions could help in various ways and could assess the level of competence achieved by each student.

This form of preparation for a demanding career has several advantages. It is probably more efficient for certain learners who can learn faster on their own than in highly structured courses. Even more important, it enables the students to develop a high degree of competence in planning and conducting their own learning, using the subject matter and reference tools of their chosen profession. In a rapidly changing world or occupation, planning skills are almost as important as basic professional knowledge and skill. A lawyer, doctor, professor, architect, or adult educator who is not willing and able to continue learning soon finds his skills obsolete.

A third issue concerns the assumptions and activities of adult educators. The basic view of the human being that emerges from many studies of individual learning is remarkably consistent. People seem to be quite active, responsible, capable, and self-reliant as learners. Why, then, do adult educators typically regard and treat adults as passive, not interested in learning, neither willing nor able to plan and conduct their own learning, and dependent on an instructor? Studies show that almost 80 percent of adults' learning efforts are individual ones. Why do adult educators concentrate on people who learn in groups organized by institutions and ignore the individual learners?[4]

Although adult learners are generally competent and successful at planning their own individual learning, they report, almost without exception, that they would have liked and benefited from additional help of an appropriate kind. They encounter internal and external difficulties that slow them down or send them on inefficient pathways. Consequently, they want and need some additional help, as long as it is effective and comes with no strings attached.[5]

I am not suggesting that adult educators try to direct the entire range of adult learning or set up a monumental system of courses, credentials, and credits. Rather, adult educators must recognize the natural adult learning process and adapt to it instead of continuing to insist that learners adapt to the group modes. We must provide fresh services, resources, and opportunities and enable learners to be free to choose or reject them.[6]

Roles for Adult Educators

How should adult educators respond to the newly emerging picture of individual learning? In particular, how can adult educators better assist adult learners?

Many educational institutions have responded by providing individualized learning resources for their students: tapes, records, programed instruction, and correspondence courses as well as books and journals. This step is a good one, but it is not nearly enough. Educators must learn to do much more than merely provide instruction, which is their traditional response.

Learning networks are another response, provided often as a service by students or counterculture youth rather than by educational institutions. If someone wants to find a teacher or a partner for a certain learning project, he telephones the network and states his request. The exchange then tries to match that person with someone in their files who has offered to teach that subject matter.

A third response, only recently beginning to emerge, is the effort by educators to help adults choose what and how to learn. Tough (1967) found that learners in the individual transactional mode consult an average of ten persons in the course of a project (see also Luikart, 1977). Though retaining control, the learner asks different persons for advice, information, and encouragement. Nonetheless, most of Tough's interviewees, even though they were college graduates, stated that they would have liked even more help. This should not surprise adult educators, since they know how challenging and difficult it is to plan and manage an educational program.

Adult educators can help individual learners choose what and how to learn by offering group classes that address these questions. Each individual learner will be stimulated and encouraged by the thoughts and progress of other members. Individual counseling programs, like the National Center for Educational Brokering, can be established to help adults make educational decisions. Finally, educators can acquaint themselves with a number of recent books that encourage adults to learn and grow by providing advice, presenting a broad panorama of possibilities, and discussing self-diagnosis of individual learning needs. Educators can then refer adult learners to these resources.

A fourth response is for educators to modify somewhat the structure of courses and workshops, adapting them to what we have learned from research in individual learning. For example, students can be given more freedom in choosing how and what to learn. There appears little need to emphasize academic credit to motivate adults; about 95 percent of adult learning is motivated by reasons other than the acquisition of credit. In independent study, self-directed learning, and self-directed professional development, educators can serve as consultants to the learners. As consultants, they would not directly provide content or instruction. Prairie View Mental Health Center (Newton, Kansas) has such a program to facilitate self-directed professional development among mental health professionals. Malcolm Knowles has developed similar innovations in self-directed learning and self-diagnosis in the adult education graduate program at North Carolina State University at Raleigh.

A fifth and final response, still only a potential new service on the future frontiers of adult learning, is to develop methods that will aid the adult learner to achieve competence in planning. If we could devise group programs, individual counseling, and printed materials to help each learner develop this competence, we would greatly encourage and foster individual adult learning.

Frontiers in Theory and Research

The studies cited in this chapter have established a reasonably consistent picture of several aspects of individual learning: what and why people learn; how much time they spend at individual learning efforts; the particular methods and resources they use; the planning steps or teaching tasks they perform; and the people who help them with these tasks. About 90 percent of all adults engage in at least one major individual learning effort each year. Approximately 85 percent of these projects are individual, rather than group, efforts.

Penland (1977) gives us some idea of the demographic and other variables that influence the tendency toward individual learning. He emphasizes, however, that these independent variables account for only a small portion of the variance in the tendency to engage in individual learning. Although there are statistically significant differences between learners and nonlearners, the magnitude of the difference is rarely very large.

Most of the controversy regarding individual learning has shifted recently from the sphere of research and theory to the sphere of the professional practitioner. Several persons and projects are currently wrestling with the implications that individual learning might have for public policy and funding, and for the role and functions of the professional adult educator. As we look ahead to the next decade of research in adult education, three major issues emerge.

First, we should devote more effort to understanding the individual learner's decision-making process. Adult learners plan and guide much of their learning. How do learners go about choosing, monitoring, and managing this enterprise? And what sorts of new help do learners need with their planning?

Second, theorists and researchers should struggle to clarify the similarities between the human growth movement (encompassing interpersonal and spiritual growth) and the adult education movement. Each movement loses a great deal by ignoring the other or dismissing the other as irrelevant. In conceptual definition and in programing practices, the two movements are remarkably similar and could learn from one another.

Finally, researchers should study the relationship between individuals' significant educational purposes and alternative futures for our society. We must embed our theory and our practice in this context.

Comments by the Senior Authors

[1] Tough describes three types of independent learning situations. His classification system and the ideas that support it are in some ways at

variance with Moore's (Chapter Two). Their contrasting views extend to the topic of structure as well.

² In large part, our progress toward understanding adult education is dependent on our considering the type of question Tough raises. If we were to take Tough's question as intending a disputation of the value of groups, however, we would be pursuing the fallacious rather than the significant. Educators cannot disregard the values of groups in socialization and education. But as Tough's question concerns the proper use of both the individualized and group modes of learning, it urges us to discover various techniques within the three transactional modes that are specifically designed to meet particular learning needs.

³ Tough brings to our attention three points about the model presented in Chapter One. Let us speak to each briefly in order to clarify our position. To suggest, as we do, that there are only three beneficiaries is an oversimplification. Of course, there may be many beneficiaries. But there is only one primary client. Others are served to the extent that the primary client applies his learning. Tough is correct that the client focus does not determine the type of learning transaction. All three modes can be used with each client. We do not attempt to classify the uses to which learning can be directed. Such categories may be useful, but we take the position that the client is the focal construct and that it is not necessary to specify the client's unique aims in order to define the basic structures of adult education. The aims of any client could be delineated as subsets of the client focus. Our point remains that adult education can be conceptualized as an interface of transactional modes, client focuses, and the three systems.

⁴ Some answers to Tough's questions are suggested in Part Two, devoted to the group transactional mode. In Chapter Four, Boyd discusses the role groups can play in helping individuals who wish to restructure certain aspects of their personality. In Chapter Five, Robinson cites the individual's need to belong and participate in groups. Tough's point that adult educators should make efforts to understand the relationships between individual and group transactional modes deserves our serious attention.

⁵ Tough seems to view the external conditions that the learner faces as the real barrier to self-directed learning. Moore (Chapter Two), Robinson (Chapter Five), and Wilson (Chapter Six) would take issue with this. Moore, for example, points out that the learner's personality may impede autonomous behavior.

⁶ Tough refers to a natural adult learning process. His opposition toward the bureaucratic and contrived conditions under which so-called adult education is often conducted is undoubtedly the basis for his use of the term *natural*. His concern, unfortunately, can be readily documented. However, the term natural connotes implicit assumptions about the human condition. What is a natural condition? Are there ontological givens that make one form of learning more easily adopted than others?

◆◆◆◆◆◆◆◆◆◆◆◆◆◆◆◆◆◆◆◆◆◆◆◆◆
◆◆◆◆◆◆◆◆◆◆◆◆◆◆◆◆◆◆◆◆◆◆◆◆

Part Two

The Group
Transactional Mode

◆◆◆◆◆◆◆◆◆◆◆◆◆◆◆◆◆◆◆◆◆◆◆
◆◆◆◆◆◆◆◆◆◆◆◆◆◆◆◆◆◆◆◆◆◆◆◆

The three chapters in this part are devoted to various aspects of adult education in the group transactional mode. In Chapter Four, Boyd argues that a group is not merely the sum of its individual members, rather that the group exists as a distinct entity that should be observed and studied as such. Boyd discusses the implications of this concept of the group for adult education, treating such topics as cohesiveness, leadership, roles, norms, and developmental phases. Robinson, in Chapter Five, reviews the literature on small groups, examining how the personal, social, and cultural systems interact in the group setting. He offers the adult educator a series of questions that he should address in planning groups.

In Chapter Six, Wilson explores two aspects of the learner's personal system—cognitive styles and ego functions—that may facilitate or impede the learner's progress in the group mode. Using the theoretical framework of ego psychology, Wilson discusses the learner's unconscious as a particularly important agent in learning. Although most educators agree that learning has an affective as well as a cognitive dimension, most educators and researchers have not considered the role of the unconscious in learning. Wilson's explanations should be helpful in alerting educators to this aspect of the learning process. Readers interested in other psychological approaches to learning might wish to consult May (1967), Rogers (1961), and Maslow (1962).

All three authors would agree that adult educators who want to use the group mode effectively must consider how the individual learner is affected by the dynamics of the group. Unfortunately, most professional preparatory programs offer educators only a superficial treatment of such topics. The three authors would also agree that educators must give serious attention to the emotional and attitudinal responses of their students. In the course of their chapters, however, the authors present and review several conflicting theories. The question of which theory is correct is left to the reader.

Chapter Four

◆◆◆◆◆◆◆◆◆◆◆◆◆◆◆◆◆◆◆◆◆◆◆◆◆◆
◆◆◆◆◆◆◆◆◆◆◆◆◆◆◆◆◆◆◆◆◆◆◆◆◆◆

Instructional Groups as Structural Entities

◆◆◆◆◆◆◆◆◆◆◆◆◆◆◆◆◆◆◆◆◆◆◆◆◆◆
◆◆◆◆◆◆◆◆◆◆◆◆◆◆◆◆◆◆◆◆◆◆◆◆◆◆

Robert D. Boyd

Many educators have serious doubts about the existence of groups as entities. For these educators, groups are no more than collections of individuals. These educators find it unacceptable to speak of the growth of the group, the pressure exerted on a member by the group, or the idea of a group mentality. Thus, they would question the meaning of the cells in the Boyd-Apps model that have a group client focus.

In this chapter, we argue for the existence of the group as a distinct and unique phenomenon. A group is an integral whole, not the aggregate of its members. After presenting arguments and evidence for this position, we explore how groups develop and the problems they face in their development.

The manner in which some researchers have studied groups has undoubtedly fostered the idea that a group is essentially the sum of its parts. Bales (1950), for example, classifies the behavior of individual members and bases his analysis of the dynamics and development of the group on these data. Although this approach may appear reasonable, we shall show why it is not.

We introduce our position by referring to Bion's (1959) theories, which provide for both the existence of the individual and the group. He observes that individuals bring specific conscious and unconscious agenda into a group. These agenda often come into conflict, not only with the agenda of other members, but with a generalized orientation that pervades and characterizes the group as a whole. Bion considers these generalized orientations to function as basic asssumptions in the group's "culture" because each group appears to embody or express a defining emotional condition, such as dependency, to which the members respond in accordance with their individual emotional states.

Bion describes individuals as having particular preferences for certain valencies. He defines *valency* as a person's capacity to instantaneously and involuntarily combine with another individual for sharing and acting on a basic assumption. He proposes six valencies: fight, flight, pairing, counterpairing, dependency, and counterdependency. The valencies of members, however, are not necessarily identical to the group's culture. For example, many members may be using the valency of fight during a given period in the group, but the group may not be a fight culture. These members may be using fighting behaviors to resist the group's change from a dependency culture to a pairing culture.

Interpretations of a group's workings thus can be based on one's observations of the group, rather than of the members' individual behaviors. Just as we can observe that the flow of automobile traffic in one direction is greater than the flow in the other direction, without recognizing the distinct characteristics of any one car, so we can observe the behavior of a group.

Our case, however, will not rest merely on such analogies. A second source of insights about the integrity of groups is McDougall's *The Group Mind* (1920). McDougall argues that a group acquires structures and qualities that are "largely independent of the qualities of the individuals who enter into its composition. . . . [The group] becomes an organized system of forces which has a life of its own, tendencies of its own, a power of perpetuating itself as a self-identifical system, subject only to slow and gradual change" (1920, p. 12).

Tracing the "genesis of the developing mind" and "its evolution in the race and its development in the individual," McDougall states that both these processes "involve, and at every step are determined by, interactions between the individual and his social environment; . . . while the growth of the individual mind is moulded by the mental forces of the society in which it grows up, those forces are in turn the products of the interplay of the minds composing the society; . . . therefore, we can only understand the life of individuals or the life of societies, if we consider them always in relation to one another" (1920, pp. 7–8).

Freud (1922), rejecting McDougall's conception that groups represent intellectual aggregations, proposes that groups are formed around emotional, that is libidinal, ties. Freud's formulation would seem to deny the integrity of the group as it defines a group in terms of its members' relationships. Bion (1959) offers a serious advance on Freud's initial formulation. Freud discusses the emotional tie between individuals and some central person with whom these individuals identify. Bion agrees that such identification occurs, but he depicts the central person as the person who, at the moment, is acting out the emotionality of the group. Members form emotional or libidinal ties to a leader or central person when that person serves to express the basic assumptions of the group's culture.

Let us briefly note some of the more prominent studies of this issue. Cattell (1948) proposes the concept of group syntality, the sense of togetherness of the group, a form of totality. Cattell compares it to the concept of personality for the individual; syntality is the personality of a group. Thelen (1959), following the lead given by Bion (1959), argues the case for the existence of the group as an organism. His position is conceptually explicit and empirically direct. He notes that members express feelings of pressure, punishment, and expectations from the group. Members talk about the group as a unitary experience.

Parsons (1951) views a small group as an action system composed of three subsystems, specifically, the personality, social, and cultural systems. Parsons presents a means to conceptualize the interplay among the three systems as a dynamic configuration. His formulation of the three interacting systems accords with the observations of adult educators who have worked with groups. Individual personalities do affect much of what happens in the life of a small group, but the group itself exerts a force that affects the behavior of individual members as does the cultural milieu within which the group exists. Each system affects the others although, at a given time, one may be central to the group's attention.

Other researchers have sidestepped the theoretical issues and investigated the phases in groups. Of course, such investigations implicitly assume the existence of groups as entities. Tuckman (1965) reviews fifty articles that discuss group development. Tucker (1973) corroborates Tuckman's work, observing that groups move through four stages: testing and dependency, intragroup conflict, development of group cohesion, and functional relatedness. Davie (1971), employing Erikson's psychosocial theory, argues that groups move through stages analogous to the eight ego stages individuals encounter. The best-known of the paradigms for phase development is the one proposed by Bennis and Shepard (1956). Although various paradigms propose different classifications for the stages of group development, all evidence the existence of the group as an observable phenomenon.

Theories that reject the existence of the group as an entity reflect a form of reductionism. The position that reduces the group to a collection of individuals is undoubtedly a reflection of our cultural emphasis on the individual. Western civilization has had a long history of establishing the rights, privileges, and separate existence of the individual from society. Western civilization may be described, from one perspective, as the recognition and realization of the individual. There is no question that modern social scientists, although not all, have supported the thesis of the individual. In opposition, American behaviorists have attempted to deny or negate, in many of their efforts, the existential qualities of the individual person. Both views suffer, however, from forms of myopia. Both fail to see the transaction between society and the individual; the individualist thesis neglects society, and the behaviorists fail to see the dynamic nature of the individual. Both perspectives are inadequate because they attempt to dismiss or ignore the various levels of the hierarchy of human existence. The individual is a factor in human existence; so, too, are groups.

Our knowledge of human existence leads us to view life as both a continuum and a hierarchy of identifiable and describable configurations. Life is a continuum in that it is an interlocked and ordered sequence. There are no discrete, isolated phenomena that exist independent of the determinations of history and the dynamic structurings of causal processes. Events flow from previous events and are structured by the ends that are sought in view of the means available. Life is hierarchical in that there exists an ordered series of structures or organized configurations. Cells make up tissues, tissues form organs, organs function within organisms, organisms compose colonies, and so on. Analogously, in the study of social relations, the individual is identified as the smallest unit of organization: individuals compose a group, groups are units in an institution, institutions make up communities, and communities compose society. Each level of the hierarchy may be studied as it influences the others, but equally important to our understanding is the examination of each in its own right. If we are to study groups, we cannot do so by studying only the individuals who compose the small group. Such an approach attempts to describe and explain one organizational structure, the small group, in terms of another organizational structure, the individual.

A realization of the integrity of the group, its developmental stages, and interacting systems is essential for the adult educator who wants to apply the theories proposed in research studies. As Boyd and Apps note in Chapter One, if adult education is a unique field of study, we must address the questions that arise from our own practices and peculiar problems. We have long observed the kinds of interactions that McDougall, Bion, and Parsons so clearly conceptualize. We must retain a conceptual approach to the entity of the group as we review the research studies on small groups designed by sociologists and social psychologists. Within the context of our conceptual approach, we can determine which findings from other disciplines are appropriate to our purposes.

In identifying the problems and concerns of small groups, we will focus on the social system of the group. This aspect of group life has been generally overlooked or seriously misunderstood. As we have noted, many adult educators have considered the group as a collection of individual members. An understanding of the nature and dynamics of the group's social system, however, is essential to our comprehension of small groups as a transactional mode in adult education.

Most adult educators who have been involved with small groups are aware that changes occur in these groups over time. True, the individuals are changing, but an observer senses that something else is happening. Do groups chang ? Are there patterns or even developmental phases in the gro ɔ's social system? Bales and Strodtbeck (1951), Bennis (1964), Davie (1971), Slater (1966), and Tucker (1973) present convincing evidence that the social systems of small groups pass through definable phases. Adult educators who use the small group as a transactional mode need to be aware of the developmental phases that their instructional groups must traverse. If our aim is to develop autonomy for all within the educational enterprise, we must help adult learners to understand and to further the phase development of their learning group's social system.

Groups exert influence on group members, as every experienced teacher knows. Asch's (1952) experiment shows how persons tend to yield their judgment to the pressure of the group. Groups develop norms, and members who question or oppose these norms are seen by other members as deviants (Festinger and Aronson, 1960). Teachers sometimes use group norms and pressures to persuade dissenting students or suppress opposition. Thus the pressures exerted by the social system can be used destructively against individual members. As educators, we must also consider how to use group pressure constructively. How can groups develop and employ norms that enhance the growth of the individual members and respect their rights? If we use the group as an educational transactional mode, we must learn how to help our groups develop social systems that allow constructive interplay between the needs of the individual member and the requirements of the group.

Most adult educators who work in the group mode speak about their attempts to develop cohesiveness. Their premise is that in a group that is friendly, relaxed, and trusting, the members can speak openly and honestly, feeling free to discuss their ideas and sentiments without fear of disapproval or censure. This perception is supported only in part by empirical studies. Cohesiveness must be considered in relation to the character of the group's norms (Seashore, 1954). If the norms encourage openness, then a sense of cohesiveness will further that quality. If the norms are antithetical to growth, such as a norm of low productivity, then cohesiveness will only cement the unproductiveness of the group. In groups that have as a norm an agreement not to openly challenge contributions, cohesiveness prevents significant growth for the individual members of the group and the social system itself.

A particularly influential norm is the group's attitude toward leadership. A common assumption is that the instructor of the adult group leads the group. Research studies have shown that this is only partially true. Gibb (1965), after an extensive review of the literature, concludes that the leader is as much influenced by the group as the leader may influence the group. The task before those adult educators who wish to understand leadership in small groups is to become aware of the many dynamics that interact with leadership and the general patterns of these dynamics. Fiedler and Meuwese (1963) conclude that a leader influences the effectiveness of a group only if the group is cohesive. Using the theory and observations made by Bion (1959), Stock and Thelen (1958) conclude that no constructive problem solving or work on tasks can take place while the group is struggling with its dependency relationships to the leader. Bennis and Shepard (1956) point out that when the group is in a dependency phase, it is extremely difficult for an instructor to share the power of decision making; the group is not ready to assume such power at this phase of its development. Siroka, Siroka, and Schloss (1971) report that little work is accomplished during the period when the group is establishing trust. An instructor can hold control of the group, but at the cost of group commitments (feelings of individual involvement in and responsibility for group actions) and group productivity (Kahn and Katz, 1960).

The flow and patterns of communication in small groups are also of central concern to the adult instructor. The major portion of educational transactions uses verbal communication as the predominant mode of interaction. Questions about verbal communication in small groups that concern adult educators include the following: Why do some adults fail to accurately hear what is said? Why do many adult learners who have no difficulties expressing their thoughts outside of groups have difficulty doing so in groups? Why are certain persons spoken to, while others are apparently ignored?

The idiosyncrasies of a group's members explain certain aspects of the group's communication patterns, but it is necessary also to consider the character of the group's social system. Walztawick, Beavin, and Jackson (1967) demonstrate that the way in which members understand the content of a discussion is strongly influenced by the relationships among people in the group. The context set by the developing social system provides a framework in which the particular meaning of an utterance is interpreted. When a group is establishing trust, the statement "You are absolutely wrong" carries a different message to the group than it would once trust has developed in the group.

At various points in a group's life, certain tasks must be undertaken, and specific members assume identifiable roles. Researchers have defined several roles that members adopt: task leader, social-emotional leader, facilitator, and idea person. Slater (1955) reports that task leaders are less effective and less liked in low socioeconomic status groups than task leaders in high socioeconomic status groups. (On roles, see also Benne and Sheats, 1948; Biddle and Thomas, 1966; Sarbin, 1966.) Of particular interest to educators are questions concerning the relationship between roles and learning. What roles are required to achieve certain specified learning goals? How can they be established and maintained in the group? Must the adult educator relinquish the role of task leader in order to promote autonomous learning?

We conclude our discussion of small groups by comparing two studies that indicate a direction for future research. Wilson (1973) studied the mechanisms of individual members' coping and defense mechanisms without considering the group's social system. He reports that he found no significant results. White (1976) investigated the coping and defense mechanisms of group members in various group cultures. He tested the conjecture that a member's characteristic coping and defense mechanisms are a function of his resolution of basic ego-identity crises that, at a given time, correspond to the basic concern of the group's identity. Thus if an individual had negatively resolved the crisis of trust-mistrust, when the group was working on problems of trust that member would employ mechanisms of defense. White's findings were highly significant and supported his conjecture. His study clearly demonstrated an interaction between the personal and social systems. Where Wilson, studying systems in isolation did not find significant results, White, studying the interdependent systems, did. This difference suggests that researchers and educators must continue to conceptualize the group as a structural entity composed of interacting systems.

Chapter Five

◆◆◆◆◆◆◆◆◆◆◆◆◆◆◆◆◆◆◆◆◆◆◆◆◆
◆◆◆◆◆◆◆◆◆◆◆◆◆◆◆◆◆◆◆◆◆◆◆◆◆

Group Transactional Mode and Community Client Focus

◆◆◆◆◆◆◆◆◆◆◆◆◆◆◆◆◆◆◆◆◆◆◆◆◆
◆◆◆◆◆◆◆◆◆◆◆◆◆◆◆◆◆◆◆◆◆◆◆◆◆

Russell D. Robinson

The model Boyd and Apps present in Chapter One contains a cell that denotes the group transactional mode with a community client focus. In this chapter, we pose some of the foundational questions about the use of the group transactional mode for community purposes. Our conception of community purposes is based on Hiemstra's definition of a *community* as a "geographical unit of people organized in such a manner that the fulfillment of normal, daily living needs will be met" (1976, p. 67).[1] We consider in turn each of the three systems—personal, social, and cultural—reviewing the pertinent literature and highlighting fundamental questions and foundational considerations.

The group transactional mode is the method favored by adult educators interested in providing learning experiences that will affect community affairs. Examples of programs that use this mode to influence community action include the efforts of such voluntary organizations as the League of Women Voters, the Parent-Teacher Association, the Foreign Policy Association, and the World Affairs Council. Publicly supported adult education agencies also use the group mode to attain community ends. For example, the Cooperative Extension Service regularly works with groups of rural people to achieve community improvements (Boone, 1970). Adult evening schools, public school systems, junior colleges, and other groups often sponsor study groups and classes in public affairs (Kaplan, 1960; Power, 1970). Less common is the use of the group instructional mode in conjunction with television, although some groups have been organized to watch and discuss television programs devoted to community education (Johnson, 1941; Robinson, 1971).

Regardless of the particular form of the program, several philosophical, ethical, and administrative questions arise in the use of the group transactional mode with a community client focus. A central issue is the stance of the adult educator with respect to any community problem. Some educators believe that their attitude toward the community issue should be one of even-handed neutrality, that educators should confine their efforts to assisting communities in obtaining knowledge and not take a position on the issue. Other educators argue that their role should be that of an advocate or activist. Among the questions we must consider in this debate are: What effect does the educator's stance have on the educational process? Are there cases in which neutrality is appropriate and others in which advocacy is appropriate? Is it desirable for public employees to take positions on controversial issues? Should the participants' expectation influence the educator's choice of role? Can the group itself influence the educator to focus on the community in the way desirable to the group, regardless of the educator's inclinations?

Furthermore, ethical questions confront the educator. It is frequently asserted that change requires first that the satisfied become dissatisfied or the complacent become disturbed. Should the adult educator teach in such a way that community members will become dissatisfied and thus motivated to seek to change their community? The intent of programs with a community client focus is to change the community; but change will to some extent disrupt the system. Does the adult educator have the right to do this? If the educator is also a public employee, such a question may be even more complex. Yet the alternative, to abandon many community educational efforts, seems unsatisfactory. Should the educator organize groups to learn about the community, hoping that such learning will later lead participants to act in some way to change the community?

One of the major reasons for the success of county extension agents in community change is the opportunity for follow-up provided by their continued presence in the community. This continued presence serves to make them more successful forces for community change than teachers who conduct a public affairs class after which the teacher and the class members go their separate ways. The county extension educator provides a continuity of support, encouragement, and help, in contrast to the classroom teacher. Which model is more appropriate in a given situation?[2]

When designing groups that will focus on the community, the educator must consider which situations or processes will be most effective for learning. Different strategies may be appropriate to homogeneous groups, those in which a consensus of opinion exists, and heterogeneous groups in which members meet to argue and debate issues. Although the members meet primarily to discuss community issues, the social dynamics of the group play a part in its effectiveness. For example, the ways in which a group establishes its norms, copes with dissension, and plans its goals influence the quality of the learning experience. Furthermore, members have needs other than educational ones: the need to assert themselves or feel important is one. People come together with purposes other than the community issues that are the ostensible reason for the gathering. The educator must consider how to fulfill some of these needs within the context of community learning.

Like all groups, a community affairs group consists of individual learners. Certain approaches and methods may be more appropriate for some learners than others. The educator will find that some individual's personality traits help or hinder a small group's ability to focus on community problems. How can the educator best facilitate collaboration among members? The educator must determine how to marshall the social forces in the group, adapting a leadership role appropriate for educational and community growth. Likewise, participants must be encouraged to adapt roles that lead to community growth and effective learning.

Another cluster of decisions requiring the adult educator's attention focus around the community itself. What effect do the community's norms and expectations have on the group's functioning and its developing an awareness of community problems? What beliefs about community study groups promote or hinder a group's effectiveness? How do the community's cultural norms and values affect a group's success in learning to deal with community issues? How do traditions, established procedures, and customs in a community affect group learning?

The adult educator who uses the group transactional mode to bring about community change must explore these questions about his role, the interactions and interrelationships among group participants, and the multiple community forces that affect both him and the group. Of course, one's answers to such questions are at best tentative and, in some cases, certainly highly valuational. Let us examine more carefully each of the systems in this transaction.

Personal Systems

The personal systems of the adult educator and group participants figure largely in their efforts to work on community issues and problems in the group transactional mode. Each person brings with his community concern his own values, opinions, views of history and experience, feelings of competence and self-esteem, individual needs and motivations, feelings of fear or urgency, and learning style.

A member's willingness to participate in a group effort to achieve some community end is predicated on his assumption that a group can have some effect on his community. His perception of his community's previous group efforts will influence his attitude toward the current endeavor. Likewise, participation is likely to be closely related to an individual's feelings of competence and confidence in his ability to change his community. One's sense of competence is the "cumulative result of the whole history of [one's] transactions with the environment. . . . [An adult's] sense of competence may become well organized and differentiated with respect to different spheres of activity. We learn what we can and cannot do, and we may be satisfied to concentrate on the former" (White, 1963, p. 39). Only if an individual is confident of his competence will he take risks. Related to the individual's feelings of competence are his self-esteem and his perceptions of others' opinions of him. A person with low self-esteem has a strong tendency to go along with the group on any decision in an effort to gain approval; his feelings of failure or impotence may prevent him from any active participation. In contrast, feelings of self-worth enable an individual to share his opinions with the group, even if those opinions are unpopular.

Feeling threatened or afraid causes some individuals to participate in groups, to alleviate the threat to the community, while this feeling causes others to avoid such groups. McGuire (1966), attempting to resolve the contradiction between research studies that support both conclusions, concludes that individuals who have little prior concern or awareness about an issue in the community are effectively motivated by a high level of fear to work for change. But increased fear is not an effective motivator for individuals who are already quite concerned. Increased fear raises those individuals' level of anxiety beyond an acceptable point, and they will resist or avoid the issue.[3]

Recent research indicates that adults who have strong feelings of powerlessness fail to learn information that challenges their feelings of powerlessness. Seeman (1967) studied tuberculosis patients who were learning about their disease, prisoners learning about parole, and employees learning about the workings of government. He reports that adults who scored high on a scale measuring feelings of powerlessness had more difficulty learning information relevant to control their problem than those who were more confident in their ability to affect what happened to them.

Rokeach (1960), studying the relationship between personality and learning, looked at the extent to which a person has an open or a closed mind. He notes that open-minded people evaluate separately information and the source of that information, while closed-minded people have difficulty distinguishing between the source of information and the information itself; thus the latter tend to be unduly influenced by both internal and external forces. Rokeach developed a dogmatism scale to measure open- and closed-mindedness that equates a low degree of dogmatism with open-mindedness. Using Rokeach's dogmatism scale, Robinson and Spaights (1969), report that group discussions may result in some decrease in the members' dogmatism.

An individual's involvement in a community study group is also affected by the phenomena of selective exposure and distortion of new information (Festinger, 1957). Individuals tend to avoid information that is contrary to a decision they have already made and seek out information that supports their decision. If an individual has not already made up his mind, he absorbs new information that he perceives as useful for future action. Thus, the group members' values and attitudes are important determinants in community client learning. Carlson (1956) studied a group of individuals opposed to integrated housing and discovered that these people held four values relevant to this issue. They believed the following conditions to be good: high real estate values, broad-mindedness, a community in which all people could realize their potential, and high international prestige for America. He then presented these people with evidence that integrated housing would further these values rather than thwart them, showing them that positive attitudes toward integrated housing were supportive of these values while segregationist attitudes were not. Carlson found that their attitudes toward integration then changed significantly, except in the case of the extremely prejudiced subjects.

Another basic aspect of the personal system is psychological and physical need. Needs derive from an individual's basic desires, drives, and motives. Maslow (1970) arranges five basic needs in a hierarchy: (1) physiological or survival needs, (2) safety or security needs, (3) social or belongingness needs, (4) self-esteem or ego needs, and (5) the need for self-actualization, the need to realize one's potential and become everything one is capable of becoming. Maslow hypothesizes that only after lower-level needs are gratified is a person free to satisfy his higher-level needs. This theory thus suggests that community client needs must be addressed first at the lower levels; higher-level needs will not motivate individuals whose primary needs are unfulfilled. If individuals believe that their felt needs will be satisfied by membership in a group, they will be more likely to participate.

Every individual has expectations of his own behavior and he will tend to behave in ways that confirm these expectations, thus fulfilling his own prophecy about himself. These self-expectations are reinforced by his evaluation of his own behavior, his perception of himself in relation to others, and his impressions of others' feelings about him. In essence, research shows that people who expect to do well will do well, and people who expect to fail are likely to fail, even when they want to succeed (Rosenthal and Jacobson, 1968). Further, when people who expect to fail do perform well, they are likely to discount the evidence of their success. Others' expectations of a learner exert influence as well. Educators who expect a learner to fail are likely to induce him to fail, even when the educator intends to have him succeed. Furthermore, if the learner does well, although not expected to, the educator is likely to discount the evidence of the learner's success and be less attracted to him. The results of research on the self-fulfilling prophecy underscore the importance of the educator's and participants' expectations. Adult educators and community members must believe that something can be accomplished in the community.

Social Systems

A social system is created whenever individuals get together for any purpose. Each group's social system is a unique configuration, more than simply the sum of the individual personal systems that compose it. Each learning group creates a social system that comprises patterns of interrelating roles; sets of norms, expectations, traditions, procedures, and standards; and systems of control and leadership. As a group continues to meet, the members, particularly if they have considerable opportunity to interact with one another, begin to think of themselves as a group that shares a common purpose. This growing and developing sense of cohesiveness has some effect on every participant. In varying degrees, each member of the group abides by the norms and lives up to the expectations the group has of him.

Although the literature on groups and leadership is extensive, few studies discuss educational groups working on community issues. The community adult educator must consider various ways in which a group's social system influences education for community change. A group's norms, values, beliefs, expectations, cohesiveness, social dynamics, and processes—all influence a group's effectiveness in learning.

Researchers have identified three types of roles that may be assumed by any participant in a group. Two of these types are functional for the group: task accomplishment roles and group maintenance roles. *Task roles* are those behaviors by members that enable the group to accomplish its primary purpose; for example, initiating action, setting goals, assessing resources, seeking and giving information, summarizing, clarifying, testing, and evaluating. *Group maintenance roles* are those behaviors that enable the group to stay together, to strengthen and perpetuate the group as an entity: encouraging, compromising, harmonizing, regulating, following, taking consensus, and relieving tension. Some members adapt nonfunctional roles, behaviors that serve only to meet the needs of an individual at a given time. Nonfunctional behaviors include horsing around, blocking, seeking recognition, dominating, withdrawing, competing, and pleading for special interests (Bales, 1970; Napier and Gershenfeld, 1973). Groups also have at least two types of leaders. One is the adult educator himself, the formal designated leader of the group. The other leaders are those members who are regarded by the others as influential. Rogers and Shoemaker (1971) state that the majority of those who eventually adopt new ideas do so because of influence by some other member of their own group.

Individuals in a group are affected by the group as an entity. Members' perceptions of the attractiveness of the group, the degree of group cohesiveness, the strength of social support manifest, the degree of pressure to conform to group norms—all appear to affect what happens in groups. For example, when a group's members approach unanimity on a given issue, the pressure on resisting members to conform is great. Asch (1956) showed a naive subject slides representing lines of obviously different lengths. The subject was then placed in a room with three confederates who had been told by the experimenter to say that the lines were equal in size. In

35 percent of the cases, the naive subject agreed with his confederates' unanimous opinion and thereby rejected the evidence of his own senses for the sake of conformity. When one of the confederates was told to differ with the others, but not necessarily to agree with the subject, only 5 percent of the subjects conformed to the two confederates' judgment. It should be noted that many of the subjects who publicly conformed did not privately change their judgments. They apparently viewed public conformity as an expedient in that particular situation.

Lewin's (1947) experiments strongly suggest that group discussions are superior to lectures in developing or changing a group's attitudes and behavior. People who were given suggestions about nutrition in small group discussion sessions showed a greater tendency to adopt them than did those who heard the suggestions at a lecture. (See also Marrow and French, 1961; Newcomb, 1943.) The particular force of discussion in promoting and sustaining attitude and behavior change in small groups has been attributed to the way that discussion mobilizes the power of peer influence and to the process of participation itself. Coch and French (1952) theorize that group discussion is an activity in which the member can feel he is a worthwhile contributor or participant in the group. These feelings appeal to the member's ego involvement and stimulate his identification with the group and his desire for its perpetuation. Participation thus effects an increase in a group's cohesiveness and a decrease in the degree of deviation from the group's norms. Discussions also allow members an opportunity to share and allay doubts and fears. For all these reasons, discussion is an important technique in adult education (Kidd, 1973).

A factor that bears particularly on community study groups is the degree to which the group is homogeneous (Liveright, 1959). Homogeneous groups that meet to discuss issues may simply confirm the members' existing views. Thus their discussions may lead to no community change. Heterogeneous groups, whose members hold a variety of opinions and feelings, may be more effective in eliciting community change.

This brief sampling of the literature on groups' social systems suggests that adult educators working with groups should foster a sense of cohesiveness and belonging and encourage discussion.

Cultural Systems

The cultural system is structured upon sets of beliefs, values, rules, principles, and customs that guide the conduct of the adult educator and the group's participants as they focus on community ends. A community or society may be compared to a giant egg, surrounded and protected by many layers of shells and more or less permeable membranes, some soft, some hard, some elastic, some brittle. These membranes function to preserve and nurture the community as a living system. They allow some outside messages to enter, but others are screened out. This system of screens, or filters, maintains the stability of the system, and attempts to ensure its survival (Havelock, 1971).

The adult educator who uses the group transactional mode to reach a community client faces many questions related to the influence of the cultural system. How do cultural norms, expectations, traditions, and customs affect people who are trying to develop an awareness of community problems? How can a community be helped to overcome its resistance to change? How can an adult educator foster community awareness and progressive activity? Does the adult educator have a right to attempt to make satisfied people dissatisfied so they will change? Havelock (1973), Hiemstra (1975a), and Robinson (1970) address some of these issues.

Cultural patterns are a society's way of maintaining order and constancy. A cultural system resists change primarily because innovation threatens the dynamic equilibrium that characterizes the patterned relationships of people, groups, and communities. New knowledge may be rejected because of the anticipated disadvantages of disturbing the equilibrium (Whitney, 1950). Resistance to an innovation is roughly proportional to the amount of change it would require of the social structure and the strength of the social values that it challenges (Chin, 1965). Fads, for example, gain rapid acceptance because they do not cause change in the fundamental social structure or in patterns of interaction and communication (Meyerson and Katz, 1957). Marcson (1960) contends that the strength and rigidity of a social structure is a critical variable for how rapidly a society accepts and applies new knowledge.

Vested interests are frequently at issue in a community's resistance to change, particularly at higher levels of the community where social strength and power are centered. Lystad (1960), studying a group formed to plan changes to further community welfare, observed that members with high social status and greater vested interests were less involved in planning. Resistance is also likely to be concentrated when a powerful minority can prevent or retard major innovations, although this minority may accept token innovations (Hoselitz, 1952). In contrast, change may be accepted at upper levels, only to encounter vested interests at lower levels. Thus management may officially institute innovations that workers will ignore. One of the elements involved in such resistance may very well be status. Status is derived from many sources: authority, prestige, control over others, and responsibility. If changes threaten peoples' perception of their status, they will tend to ignore or resist those changes. Similarly, communities try to maintain their identity and positive self-image. This image is usually based on a selective perception of reality. Local pride may sometimes act as a barrier to change because it prevents people from recognizing the need to improve.

In times of rapid social change, some communities may feel particularly vulnerable to hostile outside forces. Within communities, school systems are often particularly vulnerable to pressure from such forces as parents' groups, political caucuses, and religious organizations. Schools may hesitate to offer new courses or teaching methods because community groups might object (Sieber, 1967). Like individuals, communities and community organizations resist change if they perceive themselves as vulnerable.

The word *institutionalized* is often used to describe the inertia that develops in organizations, communities, and societies when their rules, procedures, behaviors, and attitudes become set. Over time, ways of behaving become routine, habitual, and ingrained. This decline into rigidity is often cited as a reason for the lack of innovation in some of the older community and governmental organizations (Gardner, 1965).

Sometimes a system resists particular changes because its members perceive those changes to be outside the system's proper function or defined mission. For example, the automotive industry insisted for years that safety was the responsibility of the driver and not the automotive engineer. Similarly, many educators insist that certain controversial subjects, such as sex education and moral training, should not be taught in the public schools because they are the proper province of the family and the church.

The perception of a great difficulty or crisis in a community usually results in a hurried search to take some action. Thus a crisis may stimulate change. Schon (1967) argues that often "only the strongest incentives can lead an organization to effective deliberate change. Something like a state of crisis must arise. The organization must come to feel that its survival, or at any rate, its survival as it has been, is threatened. Characteristically, this perception of threat comes from the outside. . . . Once it perceives the threat, the organization must immediately interpret it as requiring a shift toward innovation" (p. 127). Schon points out that the crisis need not be real. Managers or officials can induce acceptance of change and innovation by creating a sense of crisis. This view is congruent with that of other writers who maintain that the organization or community must feel discomfort or pain before new knowledge will be sought and used (Lippitt, Watson, and Westley, 1958; Schein and Bennis, 1965).

It is easy for an adult educator to adopt the stance that change is good and resistance is bad. While resistance may be a stubborn unwillingness to change, it may also be a carefully thought-out position by defenders of the social system who anticipate negative consequences from the change. Such defenders could be called the social "antibodies" of the system, warding off new ideas that threaten to invade and change the system (Havelock, 1971). Klein (1967) suggests that just as individuals have their defenses to ward off threat, maintain integrity, and protect themselves against the unwarranted intrusions of others' demands, so do social systems seek ways in which to defend themselves against ill-considered and overly precipitate innovations. Klein suggests the need to study and understand the role of defender of the status quo, and the need for a balance between innovation and stability in a system.

The foregoing summary of some of the factors and forces in the community that affect the individual and the group concerned with change in the community is more suggestive than definitive. Until more research has been done, we have few cues to guide adult educators who use groups to attain community ends.

Comments by the Senior Authors

[1] The reader is encouraged to compare Robinson's definition of a *community* with those proposed by Boyle (Chapter Seven), Wright (Chapter Eight), and Davie (Chapter Nine). Differences in these authors' arguments can be traced to the contexts in which they define community: psychological, political, economic, topographical, and blends of these perspectives.

[2] Each author in this volume examines the role of the adult educator based on his own views about education, values, the rights of the individual and the society, and the good life. Robinson has stated clearly the basic ethical issues. These issues will again confront us in Part Three, which concerns the community transactional mode.

[3] Wilson's discussion of the mechanism of defense in Chapter Six provides us with further insights into the observations reported here by Robinson.

Individual Learning in Groups

John P. Wilson

We live, work, learn, and play in groups. Many individuals see the group mode as a worthwhile educational option and enter groups to learn. The focus of this chapter is learning in the group transactional mode with the individual as the client. First, we review various definitions of *learning* and present a cognitive model that helps explain what happens within a person while he is learning. Second, we consider the effects, facilitative and deterrent, that certain personal characteristics and group dynamics have on individual learning in groups. We highlight two personal attributes—cognitive styles and coping functions of the ego—because of their conceivably significant effects on learning. Equally important are the relationships among groups dynamics, personal attributes, and the learning process. Throughout this chapter, we relate theory and research from various disciplines to problems facing the adult educator.

What Is Learning?

All educators want to help people learn. It seems obvious that to help people learn, we must first be able to define *learning*. We may then explore whether all adults learn in the same way, whether learning one thing helps one to learn something else, and other similar topics. Great controversy exists over how to describe learning. One point of view is that learning is a biological phenomenon, a mechanistic process of connecting or associating externally induced stimuli with certain responses. In short, learning is a change in one's responses to stimuli. For discussions of learning as a biological process, see Gagné, 1965; Hull, 1943; Skinner, 1968; Spence, 1960; Thorndike, 1949.) Other theorists argue that certain phenomenological changes occur during the course of learning (Ausubel, 1968; Bigge, 1976; Bruner, 1966; Woodruff, 1967). Cognitive and perceptual constructs such as insight, goal insight, cognitive field, and understanding mediate what is learned. People develop cognitive structures through experience and by perceptual restructuring of their experience. Learning is the process by which learners reorganize their perceptual and psychological worlds or fields. Learning, then, is a change in the learner's cognitive structure.

Some researchers—not all of whom are generally thought of as learning theorists—depict characteristics of the learner such as personal dynamics and conditions of readiness (Erikson, 1963; Havighurst, 1972; Maslow, 1970; Neill, 1960). They describe learning as an adjustment or maladjustment of a person in his environment. To understand the learning process, they study aspects of the learner's personality: his system of needs, defenses against change and learning, identifications and projections.

Finally, another group not generally looked upon as learning theorists, talk about learning as a social process (Bales, 1970; Flanders, 1970; Schmuck and Schmuck, 1971; Thelen, 1968). They argue that in order to comprehend the learning process one must understand the interpersonal processes within learning experiences that facilitate or inhibit awareness and diagnosis. These theorists discuss the climate or atmosphere for learning, interpersonal relationships, and group dynamics; they consider learning to be a transaction among human and material resources.

These different orientations toward learning are not distinct categories of learning theory; rather they represent differences in emphasis and focus. Except for the pure behaviorists, these theorists agree on some specifications about learning. They agree that learning is a cognitive activity that involves the use of intellect for the development and structuring of understanding about oneself and the world in which one lives. Learning is a continuous process of organizing and reorganizing what is known and believed to be true on the basis of new evidence. This process occurs within the individual, and during this process numerous personal and emotional attributes interact. Additionally, theorists agree that learning culminates in change.

Each attempt to define the learning process is predicated on a set of assumptions about man. We assume here that man is a rational being whose ability to reason distinguishes him from other organisms. Learning is a cognitive activity based on rational processes of thought and logic. In addition, man is transactive; he exists in an environment of which he is a part and which is a part of him. Consequently, learning is a process in which an individual continuously tests the realities he perceives. The content of learning may be one's environment, one's self, or the transactional relationships between self and environment. Learning culminates in change, as a person develops new perceptions and new patterns of organizing those perceptions. These changes, in turn, affect the nature of future inquiries the individual chooses to pursue.

Another assumption about man pertinent to learning is that the mind has both conscious and unconscious dimensions. During learning people become conscious of certain realities (information or techniques) that they did not previously perceive or that they previously perceived unconsciously; for example, intrapersonal attributes that pertain to attitudes about oneself, others, and the world in which one lives. These realities are consciously perceived when the individual learns to rationally and reasonably organize them for self-satisfaction. Learning is thus a process of growth and development whereby the learner organizes and reorganizes his perceptions of what he knows about himself, his environment, and various interrelationships between the two.

Researchers have tried to delineate the different processes that occur while a person is learning and to organize these descriptions into a comprehensive and consistent explanation of what happens within an individual during the course of learning. Boyd (1969) identifies two dimensions of cognitive processes: the *molar* and the *molecular*. The molar dimension is the context within or around which learning is organized; that is, the problem-solving phases that provide a meaningful sequence of activities for organizing an inquiry. These include identifying the problem or what is to be learned, ascertaining what is known and what is yet needed, developing plans to gather whatever is needed to resolve the problem, gathering the needed resources, applying these resources to the problem, and evaluating the procedures followed and the results obtained.

During the learner's progression through these molar phases, certain cognitive processes come into play; the molecular dimension comprises these processes. For example, as one identifies a problem or area of inquiry, one begins to see more clearly various isolated attributes of the totality. What one initially perceived as a large, relatively homogeneous mass now appears as a set of related but separate pieces. *Differentiation* describes this process, during which the learner begins to distinguish the various components of what appeared to be a homogeneous field.

Once he has differentiated the field, the learner begins to see the differentiated attributes as forming patterns. As he examines the differentiated attributes, he perceives various sequences among them. *Structuring* is the mental process of organizing differentiated attributes into patterns within the given field in an effort to perceive the unity of those differentiated attributes that compose a homogeneous mass. As the learner establishes unity within a specific pattern, his perceptions of certain spatial or sequential relationships among the different patterns become more precise. *Integration* is the cognitive process during which a person begins to combine various structured entities that initially appeared only as separate and detached attributes of a global mass.

The three processes—differentiation, structuring, and

integration—culminate in the learner's ability to perceive the isolated attributes of some total mass, to organize these detached attributes into some pattern of unity, and to unite the entities by formulating a new construct. The person now has a more refined interpretation of what he originally perceived as a total, global, and perhaps meaningless, mass. These processes may lead him to interpretations totally different from those he earlier held and may even result in his conceptualizing the homogeneous mass in a radically different way. Most importantly, he is now capable of making abstractions that incorporate attributes of specific entities within a given field or establish an entity that is not idiosyncratic to any one set of specific entities within that same field. *Abstraction* is the fourth cognitive process in learning.

Obviously other things happen as an individual learns. For example, during a group discussion, individuals frequently raise questions about a particular piece of information. A learner might be seeking more clarity (increased differentiation), more unity (structuring), or ways to combine certain entities (integration). The learner's internalized feedback system allows for or suggests the need to redifferentiate, restructure, or reintegrate. Secondly, although these mental processes take place in the present, they do not transpire in isolation from the past and future. Thus an individual's comments or questions about a piece of information may be motivated by an inconsistency between that piece of information and what he already knows. Memory, the repository of previously developed constructs, plays an important and influential role in the process of learning. By examining and testing constructs stored in his memory and comparing them to related present constructs, the individual places new information into the framework of what he already knows. At times, the learner is unable to recall anything relevant to the task at hand, either because he has not previously learned any relevant constructs or because he has forgotten them. Forgetting is the loss of the capability to retrieve certain specified information. Forgetting results from incomplete or inadequate cognitive structuring, the replacement of previously developed constructs with more completely developed constructs, or the excision from consciousness of that which is too painful to recall. (The role of defense mechanisms in the learning process is discussed later in this chapter, in the section "Coping Functions of the Ego.")

The future also plays an important role in the learning process. An individual may question or comment on a piece of information in order to test how that information will fit into the overall scheme or plan the individual has set for himself. If he finds the new information appropriate to future purposes, he can more easily integrate it into his ongoing inquiry.

Generalization is the mental process that is, in a sense, the culmination of the progression of the cognitive processes. Whereas abstracting involves the use of selected aspects of a phenomenon, generalization involves the perception of a common pattern, which is exemplified by all of the examples or instances. Thus generalization is a summation of the products of the process of abstracting. The individual is now capable of reaching determinations and conclusions about a construct or sets of constructs. He can see how these constructs may apply or relate to fields of inquiry other than those that are being pursued at the present time.

Activities in the molar dimension thus describe the sequential relationships of activities during which learning occurs, while the molecular dimension depicts certain sequentially related mental processes that occur as people learn. This framework is consistent with the commonly held assumptions that learning is a dynamic process during which an individual comes to know something new and that learning happens within the individual to fulfill whatever purpose the individual has for wanting to know. This framework also provides an organization of concepts for productive research programs about the learning process.

Earlier we mentioned that one of the assumptions shared by theorists is that learning culminates in changes in the learner's skills, knowledge, behavior, or attitudes. One aspiration of adult educators is to help people learn how to learn, how to focus inquiries and actions. The molecular dimension provides a guide for the educator's assessment of a learner's progress toward this goal. Does the learner differentiate? Can he structure and integrate? Is he now capable of making abstractions and formulating generalizations? These kinds of evaluative questions are crucial to educators concerned with helping people learn how to learn.

Having established a framework within which to describe the process of learning, we can now discuss the relationships among personality, group dynamics, and learning. When an individual enters a group to learn, various psychological factors influence how he learns and what he learns. Researchers have studied the effects of emotional climate (Bion, 1959; Thelen, 1968), group control (Cartwright and Zander, 1968; Janis, 1972; Schutz, 1970), individual participation (Thelen, 1968), personality and group behavior (Bales, 1970), roles of members (Ausubel, 1968), phase development in groups (Davie, 1971; Shaw, 1971), and communication patterns and styles in small groups (Boyd and Wilson, 1974).[1] Studies of memory, perception, motivation, and cognitive mapping help us understand the complex process of learning in groups. Two attributes of the learner's personality have received m imal attention: cognitive styles and coping functions of the ego. B(h of these characteristics influence perception, motivation, and memory. Within groups, the manner in which members relate to one another reflects these personality attributes. In the following sections, we discuss the effects of these personality attributes on the learner's success in learning in groups.

Cognitive Styles

Several aspects of personality relate to one's performance on cognitive tasks. These aspects, termed *cognitive styles,* refer to "self-consistent and enduring individual differences in cognitive organization and functioning" (Ausubel, 1968, p. 170). Cognitive styles are patterns of processing information that develop in harmony with other personal characteristics. They are manifested in stable preferences or attitudes that characterize individual modes of perceiving, remembering, thinking, and problem solving. As such, their influence extends to almost all human activities, especially learning, as well as social and interpersonal activity within groups. Gardner and others (1959) isolated five cognitive control principles that come into operation when a person is confronted with different adaptive requirements. These are tolerance for instability, equivalence range, leveling-sharpening, focusing-scanning, and field articulation.

Tolerance for instability refers to a characteristic of individuals who do not reject information or experiences simply because they disagree with what the individual knows to be true. Tolerant individuals accept diversity and have little need to mold experiences to conform to their expectations. Those intolerant of instability resist perceptual or cognitive experiences that contradict their conventional depiction of reality. Intolerance of instability is a manifestation of closed-mindedness and is symptomatic of anxiety (Ausubel, 1968). An anxious person requires immediate and clear-cut answers and is impatient with conflicting evidence, tentative conclusions, or alternative solutions. If a group member seeks clear-cut answers, and the group responds with a variety of possible answers, that member is not likely to learn what he wants in that group.

Equivalence range describes the preferences of individuals in establishing categories of an acceptable breadth. Some individuals show consistent preference for inclusive categories; they tend to include many diverse entities, such as objects, persons, or ideas, within one category. Other individuals consistently prefer narrow categories and require many distinct categories for classifying similar and related objects. Learners who prefer broad categories sometimes overlook certain dynamic relationships among pieces of information because they do not adequately differentiate among the elements in their broad categories. Learners who devise extremely narrow categories sometimes have difficulty structuring and integrating the many small categories. People who prefer narrow categories tend to take greater risks of being wrong than do those who prefer broad categories (Bruner and Tajfel, 1961). To question, comment, or in other ways test information in a group setting seem extremely risky actions for some individuals. The willingness to take such risks, however, is extremely important for individuals in learning groups. Learners must take such risks in order to better understand how new information relates to what h‿ already knows and whether it is relevant to his educational aims. Therefore, the group and its members must strive for dynamics that are conducive to individual risk taking.

Leveling and *sharpening* denote modes of organizing a sequence of stimuli. "Levelers" display a low level of articulation; they tend to blur similar memories, or to merge perceived objects or events with similar, but not necessarily identical, events recalled from experience. "Sharpeners" exhibit a high level of articulation, they are le ɪ likely to confuse similar objects and, conversely, may magnify small differences to the extent that they exaggerate the importance of such differences. Individuals differ in what they remember and differ especially in their tendencies to modify or distort memory traces across time. The blurring of past experiences indicates a weakness in integration or structuring, probably caused by insufficient differentiation. The magnifying of small differences such that similarities between past and present are overlooked suggests too much differentiation; this results in the creation of more isolated pieces of information than can be unified and related to information stored in memory. In either case, the use of memory for learning is inhibited.

Cognitive focusing has two characteristics: it represents a tendency to narrow awareness and keep experiences discrete and a tendency to separate affect from idea. Individuals who consistently overestimate the size of a field (for example, a learning task, a process, or a visual picture) were termed *focusers;* those who more accurately estimate the size of fields, *scanners* (Schlesinger, 1954). It is believed that scanners more accurately estimate size because they pay attention to the object they are evaluating—just as focusers are inclined to do—and they also pay attention to peripheral stimuli as a basis for comparison (Gardner and Long, 1962). Using our earlier example, we can compare how focusers and scanners handle a problem that first appears to be a total, undifferentiated whole or mass. Focusers tend to isolate certain pieces of the whole and pay strict attention to them. Scanners are more likely to isolate greater numbers of attributes within the perceptual field, including those that have only peripheral relationships. Scanners are more likely to progress easily and quickly through the learning process than focusers, perhaps because scanners are more thorough in their differentiation processes and visualize more of the total situation. This enables them to structure and integrate with greater ease. Focusers spend more time and energy in differentiating and redifferentiating, leaving them less time and energy for structuring and integrating.

Focusing and scanning also have implications for learning in groups. As each member of a group employs the processes of focusing and scanning in viewing the members of a group and the group as a whole, he will be inclined to act in ways that make his new perceptions conform to the beliefs he already holds about members and groups. People tend to organize their world of ideas, people, and authority in accordance with what they already believe. They generally organize that which is not congruent in terms of its similarity to what is congruent. Individuals, however, have different needs for internal consistency within their systems of belief (Rokeach, 1960). Some are content to internalize contradictory information into discrete compartments, while others maintain consistency by rejecting all new propositions that appear incongruent with their existing beliefs. If the material under study contradicts what an individual already believes to be true, he may simply leave the group. Similarly, if the norms and values developed by a group drastically conflict with those of the individual, he may reject what the group stands for, what the group is studying, and leave the group permanently.

Field articulation has received far more attention than the other cognitive styles. Witkin and others (1962) define two extremes of field articulation: *field independence* refers to preferences for approaching the environment in analytical terms; *field dependence* refers to preferences for experiencing events globally in an undifferentiated fashion. Analytically inclined individuals tend to perceive figures as discrete from their backgrounds, and they are generally facile on tasks that require high levels of differentiation and analysis. Global individuals are more inclined to identify with a group and are perceptive and sensitive to social characteristics, such as faces and names. They seem highly susceptible to external influence and greatly affected by isolation from other people.

Witkin and others (1977), discussing the relationships between field articulation and learning, show that styles first identified through work in perception manifest themselves equally in individuals' treatment of symbolic representations, in activities such as thinking and problem solving. Individuals who cannot keep items separate from a surrounding field have difficulty with problems whose solution depends on removing a critical element from the context in which it is presented and restructuring the material so that it is useful in a different context. In other words, field dependent and field independent preferences affect a learner's ability to abstract and generalize.

Contrasting social orientations are also associated with field articulation. Field dependent persons demonstrate greater needs to be liked by others and to be close to others; they are perceived as warm, tactful, considerate, and affectionate by others; and they like to know and be known by others. Field independent persons are more impersonal. They appear insensitive to certain social undercurrents, are described as cold and distant, are unaware of the importance of effective human relationships in achieving group and individual goals, and are individualistic (Witkin and others, 1977). It seems plausible, therefore, that persons who have field dependent preferences are better oriented to learning in groups, while those who are field independent may find groups less appropriate modes.

Although little research has been specifically directed toward identifying how cognitive styles affect the process of learning, individual preferences that coincide with differing cognitive styles would seem to significantly affect learning. Certain preferences may disrupt the flow and sequence of learning or limit the capabilities of problem solving, abstracting, and generalizing. Other preferences may have facilitative effects.

Further research is also needed to explore the relationships between group processes and cognitive styles. Koskela (1973) examined individuals' variance of cognitive control principles when they were confronted by different adaptive requirements. The results, though not all statistically significant, suggest that as groups progress through phases similar to Erikson's (1963) ego stages, different adaptive requirements surface among group members. We may speculate that, for example, while field independent people are producing differentiated structures, field dependent people will be producing complex structures. Learning, in addition to being influenced by individual cognitive styles, may also be affected by the members' ego identity concerns, such as autonomy, identity, and role diffusion.

Finally, theorists have long debated whether cognitive control principles are the same as defense mechanisms (Ausubel, 1968; Gardner and others, 1959; Koskela, 1973). Indeed, intolerance of stability seems similar to the defense doubt and indecision (Kroeber, 1969), and the preference for leveling or sharpening seems somewhat related to undoing (Freud, 1963). Theorists who propose a model of defensive organization (Hoffer, 1954; Lichtenberg and Slap, 1971; Schiller, 1958) present some interesting interrelations between cognitive styles and defense mechanisms. The model posits that intrapsychic signals, perceived as feelings, guide the activities of the defense organization. When a motivating urge produces a disequilibrium, the affect signals a possible danger and the individual initiates a search for a solution. As an individual considers trial solutions, he may arouse feelings of pleasurable gain or painful loss. Anticipation of positive affects—such as the discharge of drives, functional pleasure, and the feeling of safety—orient the defensive organization toward objects and goals. Anticipation of such unpleasurable affects as psychic pain, anxiety, sadness, guilt, shame, awareness of impaired functioning, and loss of security orient the defensive organization toward seeking a way to avoid further threat or loss.

Some research on the relatedness of cognitive styles and defense mechanisms could be developed on the basis of this model, although not all cognitive control principles are defensive reactions. Until research suggests otherwise, we must assume that cognitive styles and defense mechanisms are separate entities of personality that show certain related characteristics.[2]

Coping Functions of the Ego

Earlier in this chapter, we discussed learning as a continuous and sequential process of organizing and reorganizing personal perceptions of individual realities. Learning includes the learner coming to know, understand and integrate new content about himself, his environment, and their interrelatedness. Learning is growth; a learner does not only acquire knowledge, he also strengthens and develops who he is and what he stands for. Learning thus results in a need for self-examination and a reorganization of established ways of functioning and looking at things. It is not so surprising then that some perceive learning as threatening.

Learning in groups may appear even more threatening than learning independently. It is one thing to confess our ignorance and uncertainty to ourselves and quite another to admit them in public. Many researchers have explored the conditions under which learners, especially adult learners, learn best (Gagné, 1965; Kidd, 1973, 1976; Knowles, 1973). In discussing the psychological environment within which learning occurs, Rogers hypothesizes that: "The educational situation which most effectively promotes significant learning is one in which (1) threat to the self of the learner is reduced to a minimum, and (2) differentiated perception of the field of experience is facilitated" (1965, pp. 389–391). Research tends to corroborate this hypothesis and emphasizes further the importance of the emotional climate, atmosphere, or conditions within a group that may inhibit or facilitate individual learning (Boyd and Wilson, 1974; Janis, 1972; Pridham, 1972; Thelen, 1968).

A large body of literature on coping and defense mechanisms describes and analyzes how people react to threatening conditions. Freud originated the study of defensive behaviors, defining defense as the efforts of the ego to render an instinctual wish or impulse inoperative. According to Freud (1926), anxiety signals the ego that the danger of annihilation is imminent and thus initiates or motivates the ego's employing of defense methods. Anna Freud (1963) refined and elaborated on her predecessor's work, identifying three basic motives that arouse the ego's defenses: instinct-based anxiety, superego anxiety, and objective anxiety. She describes ten defense mechanisms: regression, repression, denial, reaction formation, isolation, undoing, projection, sublimation, introjection, and turning against self. Fenichel (1945) conceptualized a psychoanalytic theory of neurosis based on the psychic apparatus and the defensive functions of the ego. He asserts that psychoneuroses are based on neurotic conflicts, which are conflicts between the tendency that strives for discharge (impulses of the id) and another tendency that strives to prevent the discharge (functions of the ego). Feelings in the conscience such as guilt, disgust, and shame, can motivate the ego's defense mechanisms. The conscience's function is pathological if it is too rigid or automatic, conditions that disturb the ego's realistic judgments about outcomes. The superego is the province of the conscience; guilt, shame, and disgust are expressions of the superego's feelings.

In sum, defense mechanisms allow the individual to deny the existence of certain pieces of reality or to distort perceptions of reality in order to avoid ideas or feelings that are distasteful. Learning may arouse the learner's defense mechanisms because finding out new information may threaten the learner's self-image, attitudes, or complacency. Rather than attempt to integrate new information by reorganizing perceptions, or beliefs and values, some learners will deny the validity of the information, thereby obviating any need to reorganize. Such defensive behavior interrupts the learning process.

Not all of the ego's mechanisms are motivated by conflict. Instead of using defensive behavior, the ego may try to cope with external dangers by actively intervening to change the conditions of the world around it (Freud, 1963). Activities in the conflict-free ego sphere include perception, intention, thinking, language, recall, and productivity. Thus the ego includes both reactive and proactive capabilities that may facilitate or inhibit the individual's ability to master conflicts. Murphy's (1960) model of autonomous ego functions depicts the ego as a fort that protects the self from instincts and as a center of impulses to master, to respond to, and to constructively use the environment. The ego's autonomous functions include activities such as seeing, hearing, remembering, and exploring. These activities do not require motivation or conflicts or obstacles, however much they may be shaped or colored by affective experiences related to their emergence and practice.

Kroeber (1969) uses the term *coping* to describe the strategies by which people attempt to achieve mastery, gain satisfaction, gratify themselves, and prevent tension or disorganization from interfering with the process of mastery. Coping functions include seeing, hearing, remembering, exploring, and other similar activities. These activities appear similar to those earlier described as learning. Coping mechanisms are related to rational and analytic thought processes in that they are oriented to reality's requirements, operate according to personal necessities of the individual, and allow impulses to be satisfied in ordered, open, and tempered ways. Coping mechanisms allow the individual to separate ideas and feelings so that he can accept an idea that he may not like.

They facilitate impartial analysis by freeing the individual from restrictions imposed by the environment, past experiences, and the self.

Wilson (1977), seeking to explain why some individuals' reactions are defensive and others' coping, examined individuals' attitudes toward their ego-identities, as defined by Erikson (1963), and their coping and defense behaviors. Wilson reports, that individuals with positive attitudes toward their ego-identities rely more on coping mechanisms than individuals with negative attitudes. Individuals with negative ego-identity orientations rely more on defense mechanisms than those with positive attitudes. Individuals with positive ego-identities are significantly more flexible, especially in terms of defense mechanisms, in various situations than those with negative ego-identities. Thus, it appears that people with a strong sense of who they are and what they stand for are more flexible in their reactions and show more coping behavior. Those with less stability are more rigid in their reactions and, most likely, more defensive.

There is growing activity in research about individual tendencies to use coping and defense reactions. Researchers have examined such individual characteristics as age (Weisman, Ritter, and Gordon, 1971), self-esteem and sex (Lampl, 1969), and intelligence (Haan, 1963). Each of these characteristics is related to different patterns of coping and defense reactions. As we have noted, defensive reactions tend to interrupt learning, and coping mechanisms tend to facilitate learning. Thus educators can apply this research in an effort to encourage students to choose coping, rather than defensive, behaviors. Little research, however, has been done on the relationships among group dynamics, coping and defense reactions, and learning in groups.

One characteristic of groups that may influence individual preferences for the employment of coping and defense mechanisms is compatibility, defined as a mutual satisfaction of interpersonal needs (Schutz, 1970). Wilson (1973), studying problem solving in student pairs, rejects the hypotheses that compatibility is related to coping and incompatibility to defensiveness. Compatible pairs, however, reported using more coping mechanisms and a wider range of coping and defense mechanisms than did incompatible pairs. Korman (1970) compared three ethnic groups and found that blacks frequently use repression, denial, suppression, and shutting out; whites tend to favor regression, displacement, and intellectuality; and Latin Americans rely more frequently on sublimation. Korman reasons that these differences are related to the restrictiveness of one's sociocultural background; blacks are generally more restricted than whites, hence, more restrictive in their ego-functioning. It seems reasonable to conclude that certain social and cultural attributes of large social groups influence the coping and defense patterns of the groups' members.

The research suggests that the dynamics of a group must allow group members to explore means by which to mutually satisfy various psychosocial needs. Groups that have highly rigid processes and content may be perceived by some members as restricting their autonomy. Groups that do not foster the freedom to express thoughts and feelings or that do not allow deviations from preconceived plans will most likely prompt defensiveness in many group members. Similarly, groups that appear threatening in their content may provoke defensiveness. Group discussions that raise the anxiety levels of individuals will most likely create a need for some members to distort, deny, and in other ways shut out undesirable and threatening stimuli.

The theory and research on coping and defense mechanisms indicates two modes of reacting to conditions perceived as threatening and indicates the effects of each mode on learning. The climate within a group contributes much to which mode of reaction members choose. Those with a strong sense of self will most likely be able to cope more effectively in most group situations, even those that are threatening and stressful, than will those individuals with a weak sense of self. That is, the former will work toward creative, innovative, and realistic resolutions of the conflict created by the threatening conditions. They will test information against past and present perceptions and examine its utility before deciding to accept or reject it. All these activities are necessary to the learning process.

A defensive response, however, may be the only alternative for some individuals in certain threatening situations. It is difficult to say that learning does not occur in this case, but it seems that the learning process is inhibited by defensive responses that limit the amount and variety of information considered, the testing of that information, and the use of that information in future inquiries.

Clearly, research relating coping functions and defensiveness to group learning is important to our understanding of adult teaching and learning. Although the individual's learning process in a group follows the same phases as learning in any other setting, in groups, the interactions of individuals personalities, cognitive styles, coping functions, and ego-identity influence learning. Educators cannot ignore the relationships among personalities, attributes of individuals, group dynamics, and the learning process.[3]

Comments by the Senior Authors

[1] The reader may find it helpful to examine Boyd's discussion of groups in Chapter Four.

[2] Wilson's discussion on cognitive styles is directed to their effects on learning in groups. Readers may wish to apply these findings to the other transactional modes.

[3] The classroom educator who would implement Wilson's proposals faces several practical problems. After he has learned to identify patterns of cognitive behavior, he must decide how to use this information about individual learners in the group transactional mode. What specific steps should he take to facilitate group learning in light of the diversity of students' cognitive patterns? Second, the educator must consider the ethical and professional implications of efforts to confront a learner's defense mechanisms and unconscious responses. In particular, do professional ethics justify the educator's assumption of a therapist's role?

◆◆◆◆◆◆◆◆◆◆◆◆◆◆◆◆◆◆◆◆◆◆◆◆
◆◆◆◆◆◆◆◆◆◆◆◆◆◆◆◆◆◆◆◆◆◆◆◆

The Community
Transactional Mode

◆◆◆◆◆◆◆◆◆◆◆◆◆◆◆◆◆◆◆◆◆◆◆◆
◆◆◆◆◆◆◆◆◆◆◆◆◆◆◆◆◆◆◆◆◆◆◆◆

The five authors of the chapters in Part Three look at the community mode from varied perspectives. Boyle's (Chapter Seven) discussion of community planning posits that an adult educator, working with the citizens of a community, can help those citizens analyze their community and plan for change. He discusses planning for change from two perspectives—changing all or part of the social system to achieve some desired outcome and determining strategies to preserve a given system from change. Boyle emphasizes that holistic planning must take into account cultural, social, psychological, economic, political, and environmental elements.

Wright (Chapter Eight) argues that much learning results from normal political processes that occur in communities. She defines community as a polity, a definite form of government, and describes the function of the polity as the provision of a structure for decision making on questions of public interest. Wright views these decision processes as learning processes that involve three publics: interested publics, official publics, and general publics. All three publics are potentially involved in each community learning transaction.

In order to understand educational activity in the community transactional mode, Davie (Chapter Nine) raises several questions: Which political behaviors do we wish to promote in a community? What common goals do we wish to strive for? How are our resources to be distributed? What societal goals promote the maximum growth by individuals within our society?

Both Campbell (Chapter Ten) and Coggins (Chapter Eleven) discuss community problem-solving activities as a stimulus for educational growth. They define growth in John Dewey's terms, as the expansion of one's horizons and the consequent formation of new purposes and new responses; growth is the cumulative movement of action toward a later result. Campbell focuses on the group growth that results from a community problem-solving effort. He provides several examples of what types of group growth may occur and evaluates the relative effectiveness of various educational styles in contributing to group growth. Coggins describes the individual growth that results from community problem-solving activity. She identifies four categories of individual growth: stance toward self, stance toward others, stance toward life, and stance toward knowledge and process.

All five authors agree that adult education need not assume a traditional, formal structure of classrooms and assignments. Daily community activities set in the community can provide a natural context for adult education. Educators have long debated whether learning activities in settings other than formal educational ones constitute education. Coggins and Campbell cite John Dewey's work as support for the community as a natural and appropriate setting for education and learning. Wright argues that a community's political activities provide rich settings for learning.

The authors also agree that the community transactional mode offers opportunities for growth by individuals, groups, and communities. Although adult educators have long emphasized the learner's self-development as a goal of education, an analysis of the community transactional mode suggests that growth occurs in the individual, in the group, and in the community. Both Campbell and Coggins show that groups and communities are more than collections of individuals, that a group's or a community's growth is more than the sum of the growth of the individual members.

A third point of agreement among the authors is that adult educators working in the community mode must regard education, rather than community development and social change, as their primary end. Although the educational activity is organized to effect some change in the community, to resolve some community problem, education is in itself a legitimate end. Wright discusses a situation in which education is both an end and a means to an end. Her example of a special interest group's project to influence the general public required learning in order to succeed and produced learning as it was undertaken.

Several authors describe the incidental, as compared to planned, learning that results from educational community transactions. The question that here confronts the adult educator is how to balance planned and incidental learning. Can we enhance the quality and quantity of the learning that takes place in the community transactional mode by augmenting the incidental learning with planned learning? Or do planned interventions by the adult educator prove detrimental to community problem-solving activities? Campbell suggests several situations in which educational intervention may enhance group growth. For example, if a group is experiencing internal communication problems, the adult educator could help the group resolve this problem by offering a series of planned activities in this area.

One of the most controversial questions in adult education is the role of the adult educator, as an educator, in the community transactional mode. Should his duties overlap with those of a community developer or a social planner? The literature of community development, as both Davie and Campbell point out, contains many suggestions for roles to be performed by persons who work in communities. Davie suggests four roles the adult educator may assume: analyst, investigator, community organizer, and agent. Campbell differs with Davie, arguing that the roles of analyst, investigator, and community organizer are not appropriate to the educator; they are the province of the community developer. Campbell discusses three styles the adult educator may adopt— provider of information, demonstrator, and facilitator. Campbell argues that these styles provide educational opportunities for individuals, groups, and communities, whereas the community developer's style has the potential to create a learner's regressive dependency on the educator. Community developers seek to accomplish social change in communities, and much incidental learning does result from their efforts. But adult educators working in a community have professional duties and ends other than social change alone.

The authors raise several major research questions, and the reader's comparison of these chapters will yield yet others. Readers will note, for example, the multiplicity of terms used to describe the community transactional mode: *community development, community problem solving, community learning, community analysis,* and *community decision making.* The literature includes, in addition to these, such terms as *community education, social change, community action, resource development,* and *community organizing.* Some of these terms connote social change as the intended outcome of the activity, but not all of them. Other terms, such as *community development,* are used by some researchers to refer to activities whose goal is social change and by others to refer to educational activities.

The problem of ambiguous terminology is not new to adult educators. But clearly we need to develop terms that respect the differences between educational intentions and efforts at social change. Such a distinction will then allow us to study the relationships between education and social change.

Chapter Seven

Adult Educators and Community Analysis

Patrick G. Boyle

The challenge facing many adult educators is to develop a framework for analyzing the concerns of people and their communities. This chapter discusses a total, or holistic, approach to community analysis and decision making. Holistic planning differs from traditional community planning in that it emphasizes the need to take a broad view of a given problem by considering three interrelated sets of questions. The first set involves various interactions within a community with respect to its economic, social, psychological, political, physical, and technological characteristics. The second set relates to various interactions among communities and the ways that change in one affects conditions in the others. The third set involves the relationships between the process of planning for community change and the growth and development of individuals, involved groups, and the community. In this chapter, we assume that one or more adult educators, who may represent various agencies, institutions, or groups, are involved in facilitating this total planning process.[1]

The rapidity of change in our daily lives and our increased dependence on complex modern technology occasions perhaps the greatest challenges that man has ever faced. The new challenges require communities to plan for the future, as well as for the present. Communities must determine their economic and social priorities, discover methods for realizing those priorities, and allocate resources to achieve those goals deemed desirable. The problems that every community faces are certainly manifold and complex. To solve such problems requires more than the simple application of the knowledge and methods of any one field. Furthermore, the implementation of any trial solution requires the cooperation of a multitude of local, state, federal, and private agencies that have become increasingly autonomous and specialized.

The traditional approach to community planning for effective future development has two disturbing features. The first is a rather narrow focus on the specific that forfeits a perspective on the whole. Second, traditional planning methods encourage us to view economic and social planning as the specification of ends or ultimate results. Plans are important, but even more important are the growth and development of the community and people involved. Adult educators must design and facilitate a community planning process that maximizes the potential for growth of the individual, the groups involved, and the community itself.

The Community as System

Planning describes the efforts of individuals and groups who want either to change part or all of a system to achieve some desired outcome or to preserve a given system from change. All the activities that help people meet their needs for educational, economic, social, political, esthetic, and moral well-being require some kind of planning. The common conception of planning as a technical process to be undertaken only by professionals to meet specific problems or needs is but one type of planning. The type of planning we wish to discuss here is community planning by community members who seek to change, or protect from change, some aspect of their community's activity.

To illustrate the diverse and interdependent issues involved in community planning, let us take the case of a community concerned about poverty. Planners must first identify who the poor are in the community. How many poor people are there? Do people move in and out of poverty from year to year? The planners could order a complete demographic study of the community's population to determine, for instance, whether there are racial inequalities as well as class inequalities, and whether the aged poor have particular problems. Planners would investigate such economic problems as unemployment, conditions for economic growth, and the effect of taxation on the poor. Economic questions would lead planners to a consideration of the community's legal structure and its political process. How do the representation and participation of the poor in the political process affect their conditions and the community as a whole? Planners would study social phenomena like family planning, crime, education, youth culture, and the culture of poverty. They might investigate how poverty affects land use, the community's ecology, and social welfare. In studying the community's physical design, they might consider how the design's convenience, efficiency, and esthetics help or hinder the poor. Through their studies, planners would confront various ethical questions, for example, when discussing family planning.

Planners would also have to determine how conditions in their community affect neighboring communities. Are the problems of the poor similar? How would change in one community affect people in nearby communities? Should the community try to attract new industry or would industrial growth harm the region as a whole? Would growth adversely affect migration patterns or damage the rural countryside? How does family planning affect regional population growth? Does family planning respect the values of different population groups? Planners would also need to decide how to coordinate the work of various agencies within the community and between neighboring communities.

The goal of a holistic planning effort directed at poverty is the reduction or elimination of poverty. The means to that end may involve the education of individuals and groups in the community. The concept of community is most important to holistic planning because the community is the social environment in which change takes place. A community is based on the social interdependence that arises from the association of people in some geographical location. Depending on the nature of the problem to be addressed and the extent of interdependence, a community may be a small neighborhood or the entire world. The concept of a community as a system of relationships implies that the community is a patterned aggregation of individuals and objects that operates, with some degree of regularity, as an interdependent whole.

To consider a community as a system does not help us to clarify how to plan for a community's growth and development. Rather, the concept of a system provides a framework for a comprehensive analysis of the various interdependent segments of a community. Community planning is primarily the reorganization of the patterns of human and environmental interchange within the community's system. Planning aims to alter the pattern of interdependencies by establishing new relationships. Planning, however, is effective only if it considers the entire community system, not just one or two components.

Before identifying the major elements of the community's interdependent system of relationships, we must emphasize that all such elements operate within an environment of values and actions. Values are the criteria or standards a community uses in making decisions about goals. For example, economic data, such as employment statistics, might suggest the need for an industrial park in a community. The criterion or standard by which the community would decide this issue might include a strong feeling about preserving the environment and a desire to limit growth. This community would reject the suggestion, giving the economic goal low priority. Given a choice among several alternatives, a community will select those actions that help to further the community's values.

Holistic community planning is concerned with both the conscious selection among ends and the conscious selection among means to achieve those ends. Such selection cannot be based on the consideration of facts alone. Community values and beliefs must be incorporated in the decision process. Holistic community planning requires that we make explicit the values upon which we predicate our goals, means, and actions and that we formulate our plans to consider their effect on the entire community system. Insofar as planning aims to accomplish a desirable state of affairs in a community, the planning process must create conditions for the people themselves to express their thoughts, to grow and develop in achieving their goals.

As we have noted, the community is an interdependent system; any change in one sector may affect the entire community. Thus it is simplistic to identify a problem as solely an economic one, or to propose a specialized solution to a given problem. All planning must consider the following six components of the community system.

Cultural Elements. The body of culture is the environment from which the individual learns about the world around him. This learning greatly influences his behavior, thought, and character. The effects of culture on the individual are seen in such factors as primary groups, which help the individual give meaning to his environment; language, which enables him to communicate with and interpret the environment; and roles and norms that define performance and expectations in the various groups constituting the community. A culture influences the value judgments of all its members. Judgments are based upon value structures that have evolved out of the experiences of the individuals and groups concerned. Responding to these values, whether consciously or unconsciously, individuals constantly modify and create the cultural situations within which they live.

Social Elements. The composition of groups and the qualities of group life reveal many important dynamics of social behavior. The composition of a population, its distribution, its social classes, and many other characteristics are important to the identification of community needs and problems. The social processes of interaction and communication influence how people relate to one another and how they perceive the problems and needs of their community. Social change is dependent on group dynamics, such as continuity, norms, and leadership, and the individuals who interact to shape the course of events in a social action program.

Psychological Elements. A group is constituted of its individual members, each of whom differs from others. Individuals are moved in varying degrees, not only by their cognitions but equally by their emotions, as they respond to situations in their private or public lives. Such factors as motivation, drive, and self-concept have a tremendous bearing on an individual's actions. In planning, we must consider the perceptions and attitudes of the community.

Economic Elements. An analysis of the economic effects of a proposed course of action is essential in considering the means for realizing change and in evaluating the plan's effects on the entire community. Elements of production and service enter into every phase of planning for a community's development. The economic life of a community is shaped by social and political institutions as well as people's values and attitudes.

Political Elements. Planning is directly influenced by the power structure of the community. The values and policies of political groups in the community may promote or impede certain types of change.

Environmental Elements. All planning is carried out within a physical environment that includes both natural elements, such as land and resources, and technological factors, such as mechanization. Esthetic considerations are always involved in planning, though they may not be consciously considered as people plan their future environment. The recent increase in people's sensitivity to the adverse effects of technology has directed more attention toward ecological balance and preservation of resources. Such problems as housing, health, and transportation also reflect the important role of the environment in satisfying the needs of each community.

Principles for Planning

Since today's communities are more diverse than those of some decades ago, centralized planning by technicians is futile. Instead, we must now identify and analyze the individual local system's elements, interrelationships among those elements, and the community's own projections and expectations. We must analyze a community's relationships and anticipate the direct and indirect consequences of planning proposals. Thus, our most urgent need is not for a master plan for all communities but for plans that are based on the views and needs of the people, developed with the people, and subject to modification by the people.

Thus planning for balanced and desirable change can only be accomplished in a process that is open and reciprocal, one in which all people are allowed to exert their influence to the fullest. A major difficulty in achieving this process, however, resides in the relationships among a community's subsystems. These subsystems consist of individuals and the variety of groups such as social, economic, political, and cultural that constitute community elements. The tremendous amount of autonomy and the corresponding lack of reciprocity between subsystems preclude coherent planning. Planning requires coordination, cooperation, and communication among all sectors of the system. Such coordination, cooperation, and communication is possible only if there are effective linkages among all of the autonomous elements. The establishment of such links between subsystems is crucial.

Once the links have been identified, the planning activity can begin with the discussion of value assumptions and an analysis of the community system. Then goals are set, and the means to achieve those goals are selected. Setting goals and selecting means of achieving such goals call for following a sequence of activities with each subsystem or element before attempting to deal with the entire community. Some subsystems are more receptive than others so it is wise to begin with those where the probability of success is judged to be greatest. Great care must be taken so that work with one subsystem is not pursued to the point that it is out of sympathy with other subsystems (with which the sequence of educational activities has only begun). Uneven progress may lead to conflict among the subsystems and threaten the communitywide acceptance of changes planned by the educator.

Change comes about as a consequence of certain actions taken by individuals and groups. One planned course of action may be clearly motivated by economic values, others primarily by social values, customs, or politics. In planning, the values thought to be desirable by one group or another are considered, and the patterns of change that emerge represent the interplay of all the values as they influence and balance one other.

Different patterns of action result from the interplay of forces within the community. At any stage of the planning process, individuals or groups may modify their original positions. Because each element differs from all others in its willingness to change, the actual amount of change that the community educator will seek is tempered by his knowledge of the differing amounts of resistance and support with regard to the proposed change among the subsystems. Since some subsystems are more influential than others, the amount of change to be pursued depends on the power balance among the subsystems together with their receptivity to the proposed change.

The Individual in Community Planning

The consequences of a plan to solve a problem may or may not solve the problem. However, all consequences will directly or indirectly affect each member of the community. Yet traditional community planning provides a few real opportunities for people and communities to plan their own future.[2]

The consequences of any plan in the lives of individual members of a community are manifold, and only the individual can judge the effects of these consequences on his life. We are not suggesting that we need seek a representative cross-section of opinion on every specific issue, rather that we carefully consider the varied and complex consequences of any course of action for the entire interacting system. The planning model is an instrument for defining a range of consequences for the individual participants. In planning, we must consider whether members of community groups feel satisfied by participating in the planning activity and whether they feel they have learned something. If community members feel they are engaged in significant participation, and if they feel the planning process is educational, they will feel encouraged to devise new ways to extend and heighten the quality of their contribution to a group or the community in general. Individuals' positive response to the planning process may thus influence future events more powerfully than the actual plan adapted.

Cantrill (1965) explains that people experience satisfaction through values. We have earlier emphasized the role of values in the process of planning, and now need to better understand how the values of individual participants can be affected by their participation in planning. As individual members of a group share their different values, aspirations, experiences, and ideas, some will gain new insights and attitudes. Each individual contributes by sharing his experiences and learns from the experiences of others. The individual redefines his understanding of his experiences and has new experiences in the social context of the group and community. He thus becomes sensitive to the problems and aspirations of others in his community.

The rationale for involving people in planning their community's growth and development is not to have them legitimize whatever plans professionals have thought appropriate for them. Community planning must involve community members because these people live in a community of interdependent relationships that requires cooperation and partnership if it is to survive and prosper. The arguments that different tasks demand different levels of involvement and that planning groups must be cohesive are not acceptable excuses for excluding community members. Such reasoning may be appropriate in specific group situations but, particularly in community planning, such restrictions are counterproductive. Some argue that individuals are irrational in their behavior, that individuals are more concerned with their personal goals than with those of the community, and that individuals waste time discussing a problem rather than solving it. All these arguments overlook the basic point that, if an action is to affect people in any degree, it is only appropriate that they have the opportunity to express their views about it.

Planning cannot be effective unless the planners understand how people perceive and interpret the consequences of change in their lives. We know, for example, that perception is highly selective; what a person perceives is not a random sample of what is available. We also know that a person perceives things in patterns, or Gestalts, that are meaningful to him, that his selection, organization, and interpretation of what he perceives are all influenced by his needs, disposition, and values. Social planning is not merely an activity designed to effect future change, it is also a process present to individual participants. Their perceptions of the process, their feelings about it, and their evaluations of it will affect both the success of any plan and the creation of future plans. The challenge for adult educators is to provide some sense of direction and a framework within which the potential of each community member can be realized.

Comments by the Senior Authors

[1] The challenging question for the adult educator involved in holistic planning is how to make the planning process an educational one. The reader may wish to consider the ways in which the process of holistic planning is similar to the processes of program or curriculum development.

[2] Providing real opportunities for people and communities to plan has been and continues to be a most difficult problem. Those who are in the lowest socioeconomic groups tend to be underrepresented in the planning process, yet, obviously, all members of a community have an equal right to participate in planning their future. The involvement of all individuals should be a primary concern of adult educators in the community transactional mode.

Chapter Eight

Community Learning:
A Frontier for
Adult Education

Joan W. Wright

In his preface to the 1948 *Handbook of Adult Education*, Cartwright
avers that adult education is concerned with the ways in which
Americans in the conduct of their daily lives inform and educate
themselves (p. xi). The handbook includes within the scope of adult
education civic participation, leadership, human relations, and
community improvement. In contrast to Cartwright's emphasis on
the ways in which people educate themselves, however, the essays
in the handbook are primarily focused on the ways in which people
are educated. Learning related to civic and public responsibility is
described in essays on civic leadership training and community
council programs.

In the 1970 *Handbook of Adult Education*, Sheats stresses the
distinction between adult education for self-fulfillment and adult

education for maintaining and influencing the direction of social change. He points out that living with and influencing change is a social as well as an individual process that calls for social as well as individual learning. Other contributors to this volume concur with Sheats' concern for learning directed toward social problems, yet they maintain a focus on the providers of adult education. They urge educators to foster their students' critical perspective and their desire to facilitate social change (London, 1970), and to offer classes that emphasize public affairs (Power, 1970).

Taking these two handbooks as examples of the concerns of adult education in the mid twentieth century, we note several similarities. Contributors to both volumes recognize the importance of learning related to public, civic, and social responsibility. Their emphasis, however, falls on the ways in which such learning is or should be provided by educational institutions, rather than how it is sought or engaged in by learners. The contributors to the handbooks are primarily concerned with learning as an individual activity rather than as a social phenomenon.

Our discussion also assumes the importance of community-focused learning. Learning is an essential activity in a community's fulfillment of its responsibilities for the public well-being. In contrast to the contributors to the handbooks, however, we are concerned with learning that occurs as a concomitant of normal political processes. In addition to offering formal education, communities offer other learning experiences and educational opportunities. These activities represent a frontier for adult educators.[1]

Before exploring this frontier, we need to distinguish between *education* and *learning* in this context. Education is an activity undertaken or initiated by one or more agents that is designed to effect changes in the knowledge, skills, and attitudes of individuals, groups, or communities. The term *education* emphasizes the educator, the agent of change who presents stimuli and reinforcement for learning and designs activities to induce change. Generally considered to be an intentional activity, education may also be a concomitant of an activity undertaken for another purpose. For example, programs designed to help immigrants adjust to their new communities serve an educational function as well.

The term *learning*, in contrast, emphasizes the person in

whom change occurs or is expected to occur. Learning is the act or process by which behavioral change, knowledge, skills, and attitudes are acquired. Learning is not necessarily accompanied by intent, either on the part of the learner or some other actor. Much learning is acknowledged to be incidental, acquired without a conscious purpose. For example, a significant portion of people's learning about roles is vicarious, acquired through observation of role models. Such observation is often incidental to another activity, such as, in the community context, attending meetings or public hearings.

In Chapter One, Boyd and Apps describe education and learning in terms of transactional mode and client focus. Mode refers to the perspective of the educator, who selects and designs the transactional mode through which knowledge, skills, and attitudes are intentionally altered. The client focus refers to the person whose learning is to be altered. In this chapter, we explore how the community can be both the mode and focus of learning. We define *community learning* as the learning that occurs when both the transactional mode and the client focus involve the community as a primary actor.

A community is a collectivity of people differentiated from the total population by a common interest. That shared interest may be the basis for an informal alliance, such as the invisible college that characterizes the academic community, or for a formal organization. It may, finally, be the basis for the development of a polity—a definite form of government that distinguishes a community from the population, or from other communities. Warren (1972) offers a number of characteristics of a community that may be studied: space, population(s), shared institutions and values, interactions, distribution of power, and social system. In this chapter, we are concerned with the community as a political system, presumably relevant to a locality and responsible for the provision of public goods. Above all, we are interested in the community of common interests, which supersedes other connections including that of geographical location.

As an example of community learning, consider the public meetings on child protective services held annually in each county of New York State. These meetings, required by state regulations, are an occasion for local officials who are responsible for enforcing laws regarding child abuse and neglect to report on progress and problems. Meetings are attended by local pediatricians, emergency room physicians, law enforcement officers, staff members of various human service agencies, representatives of the county welfare department, parents, and other concerned citizens. At a recent meeting, participants discussed the responsibility of the practitioner who observes evidence that indicates that a child may have been abused. Should the practitioner report the evidence, however inconclusive, as required by law and, in doing so, risk threatening the privacy of the patient or client? Or should he feel bound by the norm of confidentiality that is essential to the maintenance of trust in his relationship with his patients?

The focus of this learning experience was the means by which the community would carry out its responsibilities for protecting the well-being of its children. The focus was not the individual responsibilities of persons nor the particular responsibilities of groups, but the responsibilities of the community. The meeting was a learning experience in which a problem that transcended individuals and groups was identified and defined. The topic, community responsibility for child welfare, is clearly an instance of the community client focus.

The transactional mode of this event was the community mode; the learning was a function of the community. The meeting took place not because some individuals or any group thought it would be an interesting experience, but because the law of the community required it. The actors were present not as private individuals, but as officials and professionals for whom the community had established expectations. Each participant's involvement, both during the meeting itself and in his office or career, was a function of that person's relationship with the community. Thus the physicians and social agency personnel were present to account for the way in which their responsibility to the community was carried out and to describe the ways in which that responsibility was constrained. A community also defines certain responsibilities for parents, and if these are not carried out, they are assumed by the community. While parents and other concerned individuals were not required by the community to attend the meeting, they attended as interested citizens, an interested public, a role that derives its meaning from citizens' relationship to the community. All of the participants thus were engaged in community learning and were participating not as individuals or group members but as functionaries of the community.

How can such community events be a frontier for adult education? What role might adult educators be expected to play in community learning? Adult educators have the opportunity to help communities perceive civic activities as educational and learning experiences. By interpreting the public meeting, for example, as an educational transaction, the adult educator can help planners and participants become sensitive to aspects of the event that might otherwise be ignored. An awareness of the educational function of the meeting can prompt the principals to consider the staging, conduct, and content of the session. The adult educator's skills in working with groups make him a valuable facilitator for one or more parts of the session. Adult educators may also help planners to evaluate the event from an educational perspective. Interpretation, consultation, facilitation, and evaluation are appropriate roles for the adult educator suggested by this particular situation; other types of events may suggest other roles.

The Community as a Mode of Learning

The major function of the community as a polity is to serve as a structure for decisions regarding matters of the public interest. The community must make a wide variety of determinations, including decisions about when private interests become public interests, and how the public is to participate in its government. A community's decision processes may be construed essentially as learning processes. Each transaction in this learning process occurs in the public arena. That is, such learning is characterized by the public nature of its purposes and participants. Although some transactions may not be public in the sense of being open for observation, all community transactions are public in that they are governed by rules and conventions acknowledged by the public.

The conventions that define a community include rules that control the learning behaviors of its members. Elected local officials, and not all persons, are responsible for learning how to perform appropriately in decision making at the local level, state officials at the state level. Citizens are expected to become familiar with their civic responsibilities to their community, but they are not expected to be familiar with the candidates and policy issues of another community. These are examples of community rules that promote the members' learning. Other community rules constrain or limit learning. For instance, the local government is a patterned communication network; the mayor regularly receives reports from various officials and agencies. While such reports are public information, they are not readily available to every member of the community. Even members of the city council are unlikely to receive all the information that the mayor does, unless a special situation creates a recognized need to obtain it. The communication network thus filters public access to information. By limiting access to information, the community places constraints on learning.

The rules and norms by which a community is distinguished also govern the content of what people learn, the knowledge, skills, and attitudes members acquire. Community members may read a budget report, for example, because the budget represents a guide to how the community will fulfill the functions for which it was formed. Citizens interpret the behavior of elected officials in relation to the procedural conventions of the community, conventions that are frequently codified in the charter and ordinances that define the community. Citizens perceive voting as a civic responsibility because the concept of community permits the concept of citizen, and the concept of citizen gives meaning to civic responsibility, including voting.

Community learning, thus, is a function of a community's conventions and rules. The purposes of a community are served by a publicly recognized set of rules for decision making that define reasons for learning, assign responsibilities for learning, and give meaning and structure to the content and process of learning. In carrying out its decision-making functions, the community serves as the transactional mode for its own learning.

To analyze the operations of community decision making as educational transactions, we must distinguish the actors in these transactions. For this purpose, we differentiate three groups in the body politic: interested publics, official publics, and the general public.

Interested publics are aggregates of citizens who share a recognition of and commitment to a common interest. These include organized special interest groups (Sierra Club, Chamber of Commerce, American Medical Association); ad hoc interest groups (Coalition of Citizens to Elect Smith, Citizens Against the Pyramid Mall, Parents in Favor of Alternative Schools); and unorganized but identifiable interests (residents in a flood plain, pet owners, part-time farmers, owners of local businesses).

Official publics are individuals or organizations duly authorized by the community to act on its behalf. Presumably the interests of the official publics are shaped by and shape the current understanding of the public interest. Official publics include all units of a community's government and the individuals elected or appointed to these units; public agencies, departments, and bureaus empowered by one or more units of government to implement the policies of the government; quasi-public agencies, such as hospitals and charities, that are accountable to and constrained by the publics they serve; and elected or appointed officials who act in an executive capacity in the public interest.

The general public is the category that comprises all remaining citizens, those who have no particular interests in a given decision or whose interests can be inferred only at the most general level—for example, it is in the general interest of mankind to prevent nuclear warfare.

All three publics are potentially involved in each community learning transaction. In some cases, actors within one public initiate the transaction, that is, they perform the role of an educator. The role of the learner is then assumed by other actors within the same public or by actors in other publics. The purposes of the transaction dictate who will assume which roles; often one actor may function as educator and learner.

Typical Forms of Community Learning

We may now analyze three typical forms of community learning. These suggest, rather than exhaust, the possible forms of community learning in which the community itself is the transactional mode. These forms are illustrated by case studies developed by members of a seminar on public policy education.

Promotion of a Special Interest. When a group characterized by a common interest seeks to transform that interest into a new public policy, it initiates an educational effort. The special interest may be an attitude favoring some principle (pro–clean air) or opposed to some activity (anti-pollution). The interested public will try to enlist support from the general public, achieve recognition of their cause from appropriate official publics, and involve other interested publics. In order to gain a critical mass of supporters and to defuse potential opposition, the interested public will attempt to educate all these groups. Their effort is analogous to the process described by Ross and Staines (1972): a social problem is defined, transformed into a public issue, analyzed, debated, and subjected to political decision making.

An example will illustrate this process. In a community, a few individuals who shared an interest in the public's access to programing for cable television were appalled when the local cable franchise holder requested a rate increase, but had made no response to their earlier requests for public access. The franchise requested the rate increase to cover the costs of additional channels that were to be offered and to meet the cost of inflation. The advocates of public access felt the franchise should comply with the intent of the laws regulating public interest television.

This group of individuals organized a special interest group, the Community Access Interest Group (CAIG). To do so, they educated some persons in the general public about the value and potential effects of public access to cable television. They also discussed this topic with other interest groups, including library staff, a local performing arts group, and a group sponsoring a form of alternative schooling. From these discussions, an awareness of mutual benefits developed, and a coalition of interests emerged.

By this time, thirty to forty people were attending CAIG's public meetings. The group developed a strategy for promoting its special interest. Members familiarized themselves with the community rules and structures that were relevant to their cause and identified a number of official publics that might be involved. These official publics included the mayor's advisory committee that would make a recommendation to the city council about the proposed rate increase, and the city council, empowered to award the franchise and establish conditions for its continuation. Other involved official publics were located beyond the local community. Federal legislation regulates cable franchises, and the state government is responsible for implementing these rules. The group ascertained the appropriate regulatory and adjudicatory bodies and their procedures, as well as the pertinent legislation and regulations.

CAIG members also investigated alternative arrangements for public access to cable broadcasting. They discussed the relative advantages of different interpretations of public access, the probable demand for available broadcast time, the likely interests of the viewing public in locally originated telecasts, the availability of hardware and technical information for would-be broadcasters, and the means for monitoring the terms of a franchise agreement. They read literature on cable access and consulted with persons who had experience with public television in other areas, officials of regulatory agencies, and experts in communication technology.

Their investigation was a learning activity not only for CAIG but also for the various local publics with which the group met when seeking and verifying information. The mayor's advisory committee was both a source and a recipient of information, as CAIG sent copies of its findings to the committee and invited committee members to participate in the public meetings CAIG sponsored. The city council members were similarly involved, as was the franchise holder.

When the mayor's advisory committee sent its recommendation to the city council, it included a liberal proviso for community access to cable broadcast time. The council, having become familiar with the nature of this public interest and the law regarding it, included the proviso in the franchise agreement. The franchise owner, by now thoroughly conversant with the knowledge and expectations of all parties involved, including their understanding of their legal rights, chose to co-operate in negotiating the agreement. CAIG then turned its attention to other aspects of public access, including arrangements for broadening the use of the access that had been granted.

This illustration of community learning resulting from the

promotion of a special interest to a public interest exemplifies a series of community activities. First, the initiating actor, an interested public, identifies sources and the extent of support for its particular interest from other interested publics, from the general public, and from official publics. Second, all the participants in the community learning transaction become familiar with the rules and structures that influence decisions in the area relevant to the special interest. Third, the participants increase their understanding and valuation of the special interest by considering its benefits and costs to themselves as publics. Fourth, the official publics develop an appreciation of the arguments in favor of the particular interest and of counterpositions that may be argued. Fifth, each participating interested and official public becomes more familiar with other actors who favor or disapprove of the special interest. They also gauge the potential reaction of those not currently involved.

These activities are at the same time evidence of learning and influences on learning. That is, they require learning in order to be accomplished, and they produce learning as they are undertaken. They are highly transactional in nature, and both their content and process are a function of the community.

Implementation of a Public Policy. When one or more official publics have been charged with responsibility for carrying out a duly authorized policy decision, they are preserving the ideas of the public interest, as expressed in that earlier decision, concerning the distribution of decision-making authority and the content of the policy to be implemented. In the process of implementing a public policy, they will be faced with a number of situations in which they will be required to interpret the public interest. The educational efforts of the official publics may involve informing other official publics, appropriate interested publics, and the general public about the ways in which the policy will be implemented. The responsibility of the official public that initiates the educational effort includes informing the persons or organizations affected as to what actions are expected of them, as well as the rationale for the actions. The policy may require actions by individuals—for example, applications for flood insurance or use of new income tax rates—or actions by organizations of official or interested publics.

As an example of this form of community learning, consider

the situation of citizens in a community who were concerned about the difficulty of allocating money to community services. Both voluntary contributions and tax revenues for these services were declining, yet the cost of these services and demands on them were growing. Representatives of human service agencies, local government, and the United Way worked for two years to form a new organization, the Human Service Coalition. The coalition's charter was approved by the legislatures of the city and county, by the school districts in the county, and by the United Way, after it had been reviewed by the agencies that would be affected.

One of the purposes of the Human Service Coalition was to provide a system for reviewing requests for budget increases or new program support before these requests were presented to local funding bodies. The recommendations of the review panel were to serve as a basis for allocation of fiscal support. The coalition was structured so that its largest committee, the X Committee, would include representatives from any agency in the county that wished to join and a number of interested individuals who would represent the clientele of the services and the general public. The X Committee was to be divided into a number of interest groups concerned with youth, the elderly, mental health, and the like. A facilitating group was composed of a delegate from each interest group and officers elected by the total committee. The X Committee was designated by the coalition's charter as the body responsible for the coalition's review of program proposals directed to local funding sources.

The committee found itself faced with three tasks involving learning: (1) determining a procedure for implementing the review that was feasible and acceptable to the coalition; (2) informing potential proposal writers of the procedures that should be followed; and (3) developing criteria by which to judge program proposals. The X Committee devised a complicated set of learning transactions. They began by having the planner employed by the coalition draft procedural rules. The proposed rules were then circulated to the X Committee's interest groups and to the other bodies of the coalition for review and comment. A drafting committee met to analyze the responses and incorporate suggested changes in a revised document. The revised rules were adopted by a consensus of the X Committee's members at a general meeting. The coalition's planning staff also developed guidelines for the preparation of funding proposals. These were considered, revised, and approved by the X Committee in a series of learning transactions. The learning process continued through consultation and technical assistance offered by the staff to all potential proposal writers. Learning also resulted from the procedure adopted for review of funding proposals and meetings devoted to evaluation of the procedure.

In these activities, the subject of the community learning was equity in the distribution of decision-making influence. While a wide variety of interests would be voiced during the implementation of the proposal review policy, the exact nature of those interests could not be predicted. Therefore, the organization focused on educating the community and itself about the way in which rational and impartial choices might be made. The educational task was particularly delicate in this situation, since proposals were competing for a limited amount of funds and a positive recommendation for one program required other programs to be rejected.

The series of activities in this form of community learning may be summarized in five steps. First, the official publics identify the publics interested in the procedures for implementing an authorized responsibility. Second, interested and official publics recognize the ways in which the policy's implementation impinges on their interests and responsibilities. Third, interested publics become familiar with the procedures that they should follow in complying with the public policy decision, and the penalties for noncompliance. Fourth, all publics learn to some extent about the unanticipated as well as the anticipated consequences of the policy's implementation. Fifth, some interested publics learn how to promote or protect their own interests while following the rules of implementation.

We note that in the promotion of a special interest and in the implementation of a public policy there is no necessary correspondence between the educational intent of the actor who initiates the learning transaction and the actual learning that transpires. Indeed, the publics may learn even if no agent intends that they learn. If we consider the concomitants or the precursors to learning as education, community education includes not only public information efforts designed to involve appropriate publics but also the enactment of legislation, the appropriation of public funds, the promulgation and enforcement of laws, adjudication procedures, publication and institutionalization of rules and regulations, and the development and perpetuation of administrative operating procedures. To the extent that these are all purposive expressions of public intent, they may well be considered instruments of education and not merely influences on learning.

Expression of Public Preferences. Since the general public is by definition unorganized, public preference is expressed by the aggregation of individuals' behaviors. While no one individual can be regarded as representing the general public, the combined behaviors of all acting individuals may be considered an expression of public preference. Public preferences may be expressed in voting, moving from one political unit to another (sometimes called "voting with one's feet"), becoming a member of an interested public, and responding to a survey of public interests. (Failing to respond may also be an expression of preference, but one that is difficult to interpret other than as disinterest or perception of no real choice.) For each person within the general public, public situations offer a limited number of alternatives for choice. None of these may be fully acceptable; they require the individual to calculate the trade-offs. It is not valid to assume that an expression of majority support for a given option reflects commitment to the choice—the alternatives may have been perceived as worse. Also, those who expressed no opinion may be indifferent, opposed to, or in favor of the proposed choice, but without enthusiasm. Majority or plurality decisions are not self-explaining.

Within these limitations, however, we can identify a sequence of learning activities. First, interested and official publics identify the extent of the public's support for a candidate or proposed legislation or an executive action. Second, interested and official publics refine their interpretations of the general public's values, attitudes, and reasoning. Third, all publics identify the proportions of the general public that have behaved in particular ways—for example, moved east or voted for Smith—including the exercise of their right to express a preference, for example, voting or not voting. Fourth, the individual citizen compares his preferences with those of others and affiliates himself with an interested public if his preferences may be served in that way.

We note that this form of community learning and the two previously discussed are linked. That is, the occurrence of one may occasion another, or may result from another. The implementation of a public policy, for example, may involve a referendum, which permits expression of public preference. The implementation effort, however, may itself have resulted from the promotion of a special interest through lobbying for a particular legislative action.

The Focus of Community Learning

We have defined a community as a political system responsible for the provision of public goods to the body politic. A body politic is a collective unit; it has a corporate identity. Rather than asking what the people living in a given area are doing about a local problem, we more appropriately ask what action a city, county, village, or town will take. Clearly, individual residents of the area are involved, but we recognize them as a collective, as a unit of local government.

At the same time that a body politic assumes a corporate identity, it also assumes a civic responsibility. That responsibility, in simplified form, includes protecting and promoting the well-being of the citizenry, all the persons within the community, and the well-being of the polity, the set of laws and rules that describes the government of the community. The common interests that thus distinguish the community may be appropriately designated as public interests. For example, the community is responsible for control and prevention of pollution. It manages the disposal of waste waters so that the sources of drinking water, streams, rivers, and lakes are not polluted. The community fulfills this responsibility through such activities as maintaining sewage disposal and treatment systems, testing and purifying the water supply, controlling land use, devising uniform construction codes, diverting surface water run-off, and providing for special disposal of contaminants. These activities involve residents as individuals, but are conducted by the body politic on behalf of the citizenry. The community is thus acting in the public interest.

The public interest, however, is presumed to bear a close resemblance to the individual interests of the residents of the community. Those residents created their unit of government to serve their collective interests by acting in the public interest and determining where the public's interests lie. Clean drinking water is by no means the only interest at stake in a community's control of pollution. Esthetic values, economic effects, recreational pursuits, and patterns of social behavior are among other factors involved. In most cases, a gain in one valued commodity, or public good, is accompanied by a loss in others. The policies that control land use prevent industrial development in areas where waste disposal and treatment are inadequate; but by limiting the development of new industry in the area, these policies also limit the growth of the community's tax base. The preservation of fish and plant life in streams and lakes may require expensive investments for tertiary treatment installations, and thus raise local property taxes.

A more basic concern, however, transcends these issues. Communities must provide means by which individuals can express private interests, and thus influence the definition of the public good, without jeopardizing the public interest. A government is at the same time an instrument of and a controller of its people. In order for a government to fulfill its instrumental function, to serve the public interest, it must act in a controlling and constraining way. When government controls the people it serves, however, it may limit its ability to accurately reflect the public interest, thus becoming instrumentally dysfunctional. The well-being of the polity is constantly in jeopardy; only the exercise of civic responsibility keeps it healthy. The creation of and adherence to rules for decision making maintain the health and balance of the polity. These rules include rules by which decisions to change the rules may be made in order to adjust the balance and preserve the public interest.

If the community, as a corporate entity, is to fulfill its civic responsibilities for the well-being of citizenry and polity, it must learn to define and develop rules that preserve the public interest. The focus of this learning is, by definition, the community itself.

Examples of community-focused learning tasks are plentiful, although they may not ordinarily be viewed as learning tasks. The following cases illustrate the relationship between learning and responsibility for public interest.

Defining the Public Interest. A current theme in American public policy is the decentralization of decision-making responsibility, a decrease in federal control and an increase in state and local control. One area in which this policy has been implemented is human services. Legislation regarding health, mental health, and social services, for example, calls for local planning for the design of service programs and the designation of priorities for the allocation of resources. The planning activity is essentially a learning activity; planners must learn what interests are involved, how those interests are distributed throughout the community, who would be affected by various proposed programs, and whose interests the direct and indirect consequences of any decision would serve.

Title XX of the Social Security Amendments legislation, enacted in 1975, challenged communities throughout the nation to engage in local social service planning. In a rural community of upstate New York, the Human Service Planning Commission of the county legislature interpreted the Title XX mandate as an impetus to define the interests involved in the delivery of services. This commission initiated the process of making explicit the prevailing assumptions of public good by meeting with representatives of the major human service agencies, the county legislature, and the general public. Not surprisingly, no two agencies espoused the same set of goals for the county's human services, let alone the same means for reaching them. The discussions helped the participants recognize a range of interests other than their own. This knowledge renewed their interest in uncovering commonalities and expressing them in a new definition of public good.

Developing the Public Interest. After a community learns of the various interests within the community and acknowledges among them the public interest that may be served by a community decision, the community's next learning task is to seek a way to implement its decision so as to multiply benefits and minimize disadvantages for as many sectors of the community as possible.

Operation Hitchhike, a federal rural manpower demonstration program, was organized in a number of states throughout the country. Each state developed a proposal to identify strategies for implementing the program that would offer communities more than federal dollars and a short-lived job placement program. The new manpower effort was attached to an established rural service, hence the term *hitchhike,* and planners anticipated that local resources could, in a few years, support those features of the rider program that proved beneficial to the community. Community learning was required to design linkages between the existing services and the new manpower effort that would support the new program without strangling the established system. The focus of this learning task was to develop a unified program that would provide public goods greater than the sum of benefits from the existing services and the new short-term program.

Preserving the Public Interest. As a part of the processes by which public interests are recognized, the community encourages individuals and groups with special or private interests to express these concerns and to participate in decision-making activities. Two sorts of problems may arise from the promotion of private interests, each requiring learning on behalf of the community.

The first set of problems is the potential erosion or displacement of the public good by the unexamined or untested adoption or endorsement of an interest promoted by one sector of the citizenry as being in the public interest. Municipal planning boards and zoning appeals boards, for example, must engage in learning activities designed to identify whether the public interest will be served by proposals for the development of shopping centers, high-density residential units, or industrial parks. Such proposals are presented by their promoters as in the public's interest, because they will create jobs, expand the tax base, improve the landscape, or contribute to the growth of existing enterprise. Such proposals must be subject to community scrutiny that will determine whether the public interest truly would be served by them. The community must examine all consequences of new construction: effect on the local transportation systems, indirect benefits to the promoter, short-term and long-range capital commitments, effect on other existing and planned development. The community must compare the benefits and costs of a given proposal with alternative proposals for the same land and resources. The purpose of this learning task is to determine how the public interest may be preserved when attractive private interests compete for community endorsement.

A second set of problems arises when duly authorized officials interpret the public interest in a way that tends to primarily serve their private interests. This subversion of the public interest may result from officials' rigid adherence to an incorrect or outdated concept of the public good or from a conscious design by officials to define the public interest in a self-serving way.

Examples of learning designed to preserve the community's interests include public investigations of alleged violations of equal rights provisions in public employment, citizens' task force studies of school programs or finances, and analyses of local welfare eligibility determinations by a welfare department's hearing board.

Responsibility for Rules. Another community learning task is to determine whether the rules for conduct of the polity maintain the distribution of decision-making influence considered to be in itself a public good. In many American communities, a charter and ordinance committee periodically reviews the rules encoded in the municipal charter. This review may detect shifts in population distribution that have resulted in the underrepresentation of developing areas in the formal community decision structures. It may also illuminate problematic decision areas, such as intergovernmental contracting for services or collective bargaining with public employees, for which existing rules are inadequate or no longer appropriate.

Communities often must determine how best to comply with federal and state laws and regulations concerning public participation in planning and decision making. A number of public services—including coastal zone management, water resource planning, Head Start, and health care programs—require public participation in decision making if the local service is to receive federal or state funding. The community must determine what form public participation will take. This determination requires the drafting of rules as to who will be involved, what kinds of decisions they will be authorized to make, and what procedures or conventions for voting and recommending they will use. These rules govern the balance of power in the polity by protecting the rights of individuals without denying or unduly restricting the interests of others.

Learning as Adaptation to Change. Community-focused learning, albeit in simpler forms, has been pursued ever since people created communities as a means of adapting to the environment. In a society characterized by change, as ours is, community-focused learning assumes a central role in people's ability to adapt to change. Successful adaptation to change requires learning; to cope with our present swift rate of change, we must learn at an equally rapid pace. As the conditions and circumstances affecting and affected by the community change, it is imperative that the community learn to respond. Adaptive learning situations may be occasioned by social changes or natural changes in the environment of a community. For example, when the voting age is changed by federal law, a community learns what that change entails and adapts to it by altering voter registration forms and procedures, rewriting voter information materials, and revising local laws to conform to federal ones. When a natural disaster strikes a community, it learns (often inefficiently) how to cope with the consequences.

Learning focused on a community's adaptability to change is not designed to anticipate specific changes but to meet the need for responsiveness. The design of rules for changing rules is an example of a community's adaptability to socially invented changes in the environment. So also is the institution of a standing body, like a charter and ordinance committee, to monitor the environment for impending changes and to analyze the effects of previous adaptations. It is significant, in this respect, that communities learn to devise evaluative measures in anticipation of unanticipated consequences. Such measures acknowledge the need for learning in a situation where the nature of change is unknown, but the fact of change is assumed.

Communities learn to adapt to such natural forces and man-made threats to stability as earthquakes, floods, fires, nuclear fall-out, and military attack. Specific plans are made to enable the community to respond to particular instances of change, and general planning authorizes the invention of adaptations as needed. The community of Watkins Glen, New York, for example, developed a civil defense planning structure that was prepared to cope with the annual Grand Prix, the 1973 Summer Jam, the effects of an extraordinary storm like Agnes in 1972, and the seasonal high water emergencies typical of the Finger Lakes region.

A community is responsible for maintaining itself and providing for the well-being of its citizens. To fulfill this responsibility, the community engages in learning, the focus of which is the community, the citizenry, and the body politic. This learning is conducted in the public interest, and is concerned with the public interest. Such learning fosters a community's adaptation to change and its adaptability to change.[2]

Influences on Community Learning

Influences that have a major impact on community learning arise primarily from the social system, although influences from the cultural and personal systems are not inconsequential. Indeed, it is fruitful to conceive of influences on community learning as nested phenomena; the influence from one system affects influences from the next lower stratum in the hierarchy at the same time it is affected by influences from the next higher level in the hierarchy (Mesarovic and Macko, 1969). The norms, values, and traditions handed down through the cultural backgrounds of the citizens of a community form its heritage and shape the development of the rules and conventions by which the community is defined. Distinctions between communities are, in part, derived from the cultural context, as are differences within communities. Similarly, culture and society both influence the development of individuals' personalities. It is not our purpose here to analyze the various forms and effects of this influence, but to acknowledge it. In this vein, it is also appropriate to acknowledge the influence of individuals' traits, attitudes, and aptitudes on the conduct of community responsibilities and, thus, on community learning. Our discussion can only suggest the influences derived from the social system.

The community as a system for governance is analogous to a game patterned by a set of rules about who can play, what the game involves, where and how it is played, what constitutes winning, and how to keep score. The rules identify the game and the differences between what is part of the game and what is coincidental random activity. Every body politic is governed by a set of rules that were developed by the people founding the polity. Other rules and structures, however, also influence community learning. The larger units of government of which the community is a part and the formal organizations that are created to serve public and private purposes have rules. In addition, informal rules emerge that describe appropriate action in particular situations. These role prescriptions or normative conventions are not tied to a decision structure, such as an organization or unit of government, but apply to social situations that transcend the formal structures.

Ostrom and Ostrom (1972), in a workbook on public choice theory and research, propose a conceptual framework for categorizing the rules that organize public decisions. They label any enduring and relatively formalized set of rules a *decision structure*. The legislative process of the U.S. Congress is such a decision structure, as is the functioning of a family court or a government bureaucracy.

They depict five categories of decision rules. Boundary rules designate those actors eligible to participate in or utilize a decision structure and those who are not. Eligibility includes the costs associated with inclusion, such as achieving a particular credential or devoting a specified amount of time, and the costs of exit, if any. Scope rules define the range of actions or topics that the decision structure is authorized to handle. These rules, for example, prohibit a civil court from hearing criminal cases and limit a city council's jurisdiction to those public functions of the municipality authorized by state law.

A third category of rules codifies the positions in decision making, each of which is circumscribed by duties and expectations. In the family decision structure, the position of parent is legally and culturally differentiated from that of child. A legislative decision structure includes positions of citizen, voter, elected official, committee member, lobbyist, staff member, chair, and clerk. Some structures are more differentiated than others; some positions appear in more than one structure.

Procedural rules describe the actions that are available to each position at each stage in the decision-making process. The rules for amending an organization's constitution and by-laws are one relatively formal set of procedural rules. Each position in that organization has one or more available procedural options at each stage of the process: during the initiation of interest in amending the constitution, as the possible changes are considered, at the point of formulating the choices to be recommended, and at the stage of referendum or voting on proposed amendments. Procedural rules are systematic and regularized guidelines for dealing with various kinds of decision making. The rules refer to classes of decisions and serve a humanistic purpose. They also tell how to select, organize, and process information relevant to the kinds of choice situations that can be anticipated (Ostrom and Ostrom, 1972).

The final group of decision rules are the voting or aggregation rules, the conventions by which a decision is known to have been reached. A common voting rule is majority rule, in which the votes of all position holders eligible to vote are counted and the alternative selected by more than half of the voters is identified. Another aggregation rule is consensus, in which only opposing positions are noted. A hierarchical voting rule prescribes that the action to be taken is determined by the highest position acting in the decision structure.

Decision rules and structures are essential to community learning. It would be impossible to learn what was happening in the public arena, to understand and interpret the behaviors of the various publics, if there were no rules to limit, constraint, and define behavior. If public activities are not patterned by rules, but are only random, community learning would have no meaning.

An example will serve to illustrate how community rules operate. The joint education committee of a state legislature was considering two bills; one had been introduced in the state senate, the other in the assembly. These bills proposed new formulas for state cost-sharing in local public school financing. The committee ordered a series of hearings to be held in several locations throughout the state. The schedule was published weeks in advance of the first session, as required by long-standing procedural rules, and the public was invited to request time to speak at the sessions.

Thus, even before any hearings were held the implicit and explicit decision rules governing committee hearings affected community learning. These rules circumscribed who was to learn. Since the hearings were ordered by a joint committee, staff and representatives from both legislative houses were expected to attend; the proceedings were distributed to all committee members and made available to other legislators and their staffs. The hearing, however, was not simply an opportunity for decision makers to learn how the public felt. They would also learn which publics were interested enough in the issue to request time to testify at the hearing.

These rules appear to be designed to discourage uninformed and irrelevant participation by the general public, and they appear to work quite well. While notice of a public hearing is widely published, the general public has little reason to look for a small formal notice in the daily newspaper or to request information on the status of a legislative committee's work. Furthermore, the general public has little if any prior experience with hearings; its members do not interpret the notice as an opportunity to participate.

A hearing, of course, is governed by conventions. The content and order of opening statements, the procedural rules for the hearing, the order of events, the disposition of written documents, the order of testimony—all these actions are prescribed by rules. The rules of a hearing have several influences on learning. Statements and testimony are formal, often technical, and documented in some detail. Such testimony is meaningful to the committee members, their staff, school administrators, and other state officials, but it is not easily comprehended by persons inexperienced in legislative affairs. The language of the hearing thus restricts who may learn from the proceedings.

The rules governing the asking of questions also affect learning. Such rules allow only the hearing's officials to question individual speakers; debate between persons testifying and the asking of questions by persons attending the hearing are not permitted. The hearing's officials have the opportunity to respond selectively to the arguments presented and to emphasize the points they consider important. The persons testifying at the hearing cannot use the hearing as an opportunity to influence the committee, other presenters, or the audience except through their informal statements and answers to questions, if any. Much as in a court of law, the facts and feelings allowed into evidence in this public arena are constrained by rules. Observers' access to information is limited to that which is presented, and their interpretation of this information is shaped by their previous familiarity with the subject matter and the procedural strategies of the hearing's officials. Transaction, the development of ideas, and negotiation are not part of this learning event. The rules that make learning possible at the same time impose limits on who learns what and how one learns. The rules by which a community operates, those formally codified in law and those informally understood by convention, create order and facilitate learning. These decision rules and structures, however, also restrict learning, as we have observed.

Implications of Community Learning for Adult Educators

Community learning is an unexplored frontier for adult educators. Little work has been done to conceptualize the nature of the community learning process, identify and analyze various forms of community learning, design and evaluate strategies by which such learning can be facilitated, or to relate community learning to the established forms and focuses of adult education. While considerable attention has been given to programs that educate persons to understand the nature of a community and its operation, little emphasis has been placed on studying and conceptualizing naturalistic community learning.

When informal community learning is viewed as part of adult education, events and processes that we often take for granted as part of our everyday experience gain new significance. Participants in community learning transactions no longer appear merely as individuals, but as members of one or another public who participate in community activities that offer learning experiences. The community, as a transactional mode of learning, focuses on learning tasks related to the public interest.

Once educators become aware of community learning, we are challenged to provide conceptual clarity and specificity concerning this form of education. Labels and definitions, however, are not enough; neither can the conceptual task that confronts us be approached simply by armchair reflection on the experiences of living. Our call is a call for both research and intervention.

Research is central to increasing our understanding of community learning. The dimensions of the model proposed by Boyd and Apps in Chapter One suggest a number of topics for research. Considering the community as a transactional mode, we may ask: Whose learning is an indicator of or instrumental to community learning? What form of involvement by which publics is significant for what types of learning? Does the sequence of transactions among publics make a difference in the results of the learning process? One could develop a long-term research program to trace the effect on community learning of alternatives in each set of decision rules. Another subject for research is the evaluation of the effectiveness of alternative learning transactions for particular community learning tasks.

A particularly opportune occasion for research on community learning is the current national emphasis on local planning. Spurred by federal policies to localize planning responsibility, communities are planning for human services, water resource development, economic development, land use, and urban renewal. If planning is a process for determining appropriate future action through a sequence of choices, then it is clearly a learning task. Research studies of the ways that communities plan and the relationship of these planning styles to learning could examine mode, focus, and decision rules, or any combination of these dimensions. Similarly, mandated public involvement in planning and decision making represents an opportunity for research on community learning. Researchers could explore which publics participate, the form and extent of their involvement, and the nature of learning attributable to public involvement.

A number of hypotheses may be derived from the study of naturalistic learning. These hypotheses and observations may form the bases for the design of strategic interventions in the learning process. Adult educators who do not wish to be confined by educational programing traditions may design and evaluate strategies for community learning. In consultation with persons experienced in community development, they could organize field trials of techniques and methods to improve the quality, extent, and distribution of learning. The emphasis of such efforts would be to develop a theory of learning, not a theory of social action.

One of the assumptions of our public school system is that formal education in civics is a prerequisite to adult competency in civic responsibility, in civic literacy, to use Ziegler's (1974) term. The validity of this assumption is questionable, given the lack of interest and participation in community affairs by a large portion of the American adult population. It may be that the formal schooling of children and youth is necessary, but not sufficient, and that public school civic education must be supplemented by continuing civic education for adults. On that postulate rests the League of Women Voters' extensive educational program. The success of such continuing education may, of course, be limited to those persons who find themselves involved in the political processes of their community and who are motivated to learn more about the ways their community works.

Traditional educational programs on social and political responsibility may well play a significant role in increasing civic literacy. The relationship between such education and active participation in community learning, however, cannot be assumed or left to chance. The real challenge to adult educators is to find ways to stimulate, reinforce, and promote the processes by which community learning naturally occurs.

Community learning is neither a trivial phenomenon nor an esoteric interest. It is a process essential to the maintenance and balance of individual and social freedom, and to the survival of a democratic society. By reversing the forces that mount apathy on ignorance, educators may develop adult learners' awareness, participation, and increasing capability in community affairs.

Comments by the Senior Authors

[1] Wright discusses naturalistic education, that which occurs normally as the part of everyday human activity, in this case community political activity. She also talks about incidental learning, that which occurs without any planning. The reader may wish to consult the introduction to Part Three for further clarification of these terms.

[2] The reader may wish to examine Wright's assumption that a community creates a polity to maintain itself and provide for the well-being of

its citizens. Many political structures in this country have not been equally concerned about all members of their communities. Many polities protect well-being of only those citizens with political power or those with economic power. Can adult educators help communities to better understand the interests of all the citizens?

Chapter Nine

Group Transactions
in Communities

Lynn E. Davie

In the first chapter of this book, Boyd and Apps define one cell of
their model in which the learning transactions take place in groups
and the client focus of the educational program is the community.
In this cell, we find many of the programs that have traditionally
been called community development. Community development
programs offer educational transactions within existing community groups, such as development associations, chambers of commerce, church study groups, or through the formation of groups
designed specifically for community development activities. Examples of groups designed for community development programs
include extension study groups, advisory councils, and, on some
occasions, nonprofit organizations.

Let us begin our discussion of adult education in the group

transactional mode with a community client focus by defining several terms and examining the goals of such educational programs. *Group* refers to a collection of individuals who have several face-to-face meetings to facilitate their goal of learning skills or information that they believe will be of benefit to the larger community. We are here concerned only with groups that have a relatively stable membership; occasional groupings of individuals in large open meetings are more appropriately labeled as participating in the community transactional mode.

A *community* is a collection of individuals who share a common identity, similar goals, common values and aspirations, and who see their individual futures as interdependent on certain transactions. A community usually includes more than one group and thus, includes the dynamics common to negotiation and conflict among groups. The identity of a community may be geographical, such as a neighborhood, town, or city; or its identity may be based on a common tradition, such as the community of scholars. The necessary criterion for community is the interdependence of member individuals in the creation of a positively valued future.

The general purpose of community educational groups is the achievement of valued community goals through the learning of knowledge, attitudes, and skills by individuals acting within potent community roles. As Boyd and Apps indicate, the goal is growth, growth for individuals so that they can become more effective community members. In addition to this general purpose, these educational programs have more specific goals. Indeed, such programs often have multiple goals because individual members or groups hold several goals, some of which may be conflicting. Consider a program that includes three different community groups, an agency that has community development goals, and an agent hired by the agency to work with the community groups. The participants in this program may have conflicting sets of educational goals or a single set of congruent goals.

Often, the first problem for an educator in these programs is to help various community groups, including his own agency, to choose among conflicting goals. Such choices require the educator to consider several broad, difficult questions, both philosophical and pragmatic: What is the nature of society? Which political be-

haviors do we wish to promote? What common goals do we wish to
strive for? What is the good life? What is our vision of our future as
a nation, a community, or a neighborhood? How are our resources
to be distributed? What are our responsibilities to one another?
What social goals promote the growth of individuals within our
society? For all educational programs such questions are important; for community education, the answers to these questions are
the critical assumptions upon which all other educational decisions
rest.

   The adult educator must also decide the role appropriate to
the agency he represents: What are the purposes of the agency?
Which roles in society should it play—impartial observer or leader?
Should the agency's goals be modified to fit the interests or needs
of the specific community groups with which the agent is working?
Community development agents or consultants are often caught
between the goals expressed by communities and those of the
agency they represent. These educators must clarify their duties
and loyalties in order to negotiate their course of action.[1]

Resolving Conflicts

   Because the potential for conflict is always high in community education, the educator's general strategy is to seek consensus
among the parties with whom he is working. In attempting to secure a consensus, the educator employs tactics that minimize conflict. For example, he can treat the differences of opinion as a
problem-solving task that requires rational decision making based
on sufficient information. Biddle and Biddle (1965) describe one of
the better examples of this approach. Consensual strategies have
benefited from techniques such as values clarification (Simon,
Howe, and Kirschenbaum, 1972) and the Delphi technique
(Brown, 1968; Helmer, 1966).

   A second strategy that may be employed by the community
educator is to strengthen the less powerful groups in the community and enable them to compete more effectively for the society's
scarce resources. Intermediate goals for this strategy include the
development of specific skills among individual group members
and the strengthening of a communal identity within a group to

provide the necessary psychological reinforcement for action. Alinsky (1971), Freire (1971), and Sewell (1972) discuss strategies of this type.

In every case, the educator's strategy is to help the disadvantaged group see the basis of their disadvantage, organize themselves into a collectivity with a base of power, and use that power effectively to achieve desired goals. The questions that confront the educator include: How does the educator know which groups he should or can help? How does the active stance of the educator relate to the goals of the agency? Do the techniques used in a political strategy enhance or depend upon learning?

In the selection of appropriate strategies, one must also examine the relationship between the individuals and the community of which they are a part. Should the goals of a community development program include goals of individual self-enhancement and self-interest, or must the goals always be at the level of the community? What if the goals of an individual or a subgroup are at odds with the majority? Should the community educator work with the community to help develop strategies for resolving opposition among subgroups?

Many community educators attempt to resolve the conflict inherent in the setting of goals by setting only process goals for their programs. Such process goals may include basic democratic goals, such as increased participation in the political process, or the development of carefully specified processes whereby community problems are examined in a systematic way. In setting process goals, the educator must consider which processes are appropriate, what information is to be sought, and who may control the process through political power, skill, or access to information.

Educator's Roles

Adult educators, both professionals and volunteers, assume various roles when they work with community groups. We can identify four roles—analyst, investigator, community organizer, and community agent—and explore the assumptions underlying the structure and functions of each. Each of these roles is involved with community groups in a different way, each assumes different goals for the community education process, and each has different effects on the community and individual leaning or growth that results.

The Analyst. The community educator who acts as an analyst studies the community, often using information that is readily available in the minutes of public meetings, voting records, and newspaper or other media accounts. The analyst uses this information to draw conclusions about a community issue. He may present these conclusions in editorials or feature articles in the newspaper, in public lectures, or in reports to public bodies. Although the analyst seldom directly involves the public in the gathering of information or in the analysis of the data, he clearly hopes to influence the formulation of public policy.

University faculty members often serve as analysts for communities, performing research on public problems and submitting their results to public bodies. Many universities and communities favor this approach because they feel such investigations are best conducted by a professionally trained, skilled expert who is presumed to be removed from the emotions of the debate and who can thus provide an impartial, well-reasoned analysis of community problems. Because the role of community analyst is similar to the role the university performs for so many other disciplines, few universities question the appropriateness of faculty members' assuming such a role.

Critics of these arrangements charge that universities are elitist, conservative institutions, that often a university's concern about many community problems is self-serving, and that academicians' recommendations and solutions tend to be conservative ones that seek to preserve the kind of society that will be supportive of the university itself. In addition, they claim that such analyses, because they do not directly involve the public in their investigations, foster a community's dependency on social institutions to solve problems that should be solved by the members of the community. Still, for many obvious reasons, the analytical role is frequently adapted by members of universities, consulting agencies, and planning groups.

The Investigator. Although similar to the analyst, the investigator often works with members of the community, helping the

community organize itself to study community problems, resources, aspirations, and goals or to develop community leadership. The investigator works with community groups to identify
concepts that need to be studied and to help the community residents frame appropriate questions. In addition, he may offer technical assistance in the conducting of surveys and the analysis of
data. (Biddle and Biddle, 1965, offer examples of the investigator's
activities.) Some agencies view the role of investigator as the first
phase in the educational process; others view the role as the full
appropriate response that an agency can offer a community.

The assumptions that underlie the role of the investigator
are similar to those of the analyst: The greatest limitation on a
community is a lack of knowledge; once people acquire knowledge,
they can order their affairs in a rational manner. Thus, the investigator tries to help community members acquire knowledge of
the community so that they can influence their elected officials to
rationally appraise the facts and make decisions beneficial to the
community.

The role of investigator, like the role of analyst, is a comfort-
able one for agencies such as universities to accept. Universities
view themselves as basically neutral, and the investigator's role,
which does not include the promotion of any specific community
goals, seems an independent and neutral one. Criticisms made of
the analyst's role can be applied to the investigator, although the
charge of elitism here seems less justified. But the investigator, too,
may produce conservative solutions that merely reflect ideas already familiar to the community, solutions that will not help the
community adapt to changing social conditions. If the investigator
is not thorough, he may ignore segments of the community that are
not vocal or politically aware. Less affluent groups and neighborhoods are often not served well by elected bodies or included in
community action groups. Those members of the community who
are not well educated are at a disadvantage in the analytic processes
used by the investigator. Thus, critics of this role argue that it is
elitist in its goals, elitist in its processes, and elitist in its effect on the
community.

The Community Organizer. Community organizers work with
the less influential groups in a community in such a way that they

learn how to organize themselves to exert power in their community to achieve their goals. Since these groups are often not represented in the traditional power structures, their goals and solutions may be radical, and they may have difficulty gaining access to the traditional centers of power. Alinsky (1971), Freire (1970), and Sewell (1972) describe the difficulties faced by the community organizer.

Working with the less powerful groups—or, as Freire calls them, "the oppressed"—involves several levels of educational activities. Often the first step is to raise the level of political awareness of the groups so that they realize that they are not receiving their share of the benefits of the community and that, through collective action, they could force those in power to share the resources of the community. After the group understands their situation and agrees that this task can be accomplished, the agent works with the group to help them learn how to organize, how to use the media to publicize their problem, how to focus their power to achieve their goals, and how to use the power they gain to participate fully in governing themselves. The community organizer teaches community groups the skills needed to collect information, to effect political change, and to participate in self-government.

The role of community organizer is often adopted by agencies that have strong social action goals, for example, chapters of the YMCA and YWCA, churches, ethnic groups, and minority political parties. Seldom is the role of community organizer adopted by universities or similar agencies, perhaps because this role can bring a university into conflict with sectors of the community that provide direct support to the university.

Critics of community organizing often ask how an agency can determine which of the segments of the community ought to be assisted. Since community organizers are often involved in political conflicts, they must choose among contending groups. Critics also argue that the role stimulates conflict in the community, and thus sacrifices goals such as growth and stability. In addition, critics question whether the various groups are being used for the agency's political ends. Still, this role concentrates on community members' learning rather than solely on the collection and analysis of information. More community educators have recently accepted this role as their model.

The Community Agent. The role of community agent is often adopted by the community workers of a governmental or quasi-governmental body. The community agent's duty is to inform members of the community about the services and programs available to them from a particular agency. Members of the Cooperative Extension Service serve this function by providing communities with the results of university research in agriculture, home economics, and youth education. Research foundations and associations concerned with health, drug abuse, alcoholism, and family relations often employ community agents to inform the public of recent research findings and local services. Their agents may speak to community groups and schools, write informative newspaper columns, and encourage groups and individuals to enroll in specific educational programs. The community agent is charged by the agency to carry out the specific goals of the agency in the community to which he is assigned. He is not expected to organize community groups for political action nor to become directly involved in community studies, although he may help the researchers of the parent agency conduct a community study.

Critics of this role note the limitations imposed on the agent by the agency's goals. Agents are expected to promote the programs of the parent agency even though such programs do not seem appropriate for a specific community. Furthermore, the agent's work does not in and of itself strengthen the community's abilities to govern itself. Seldom does an agency help the community critically appraise the information provided, and seldom is the community group encouraged to become less dependent upon the parent agency. Community agents treat the community group as consumers of information and services, but they do not help the community to become self-sufficient suppliers of information and services.

The role of community agent, like those of analyst and investigator with which it is often linked, is one that can be adopted with ease by organizations that view themselves as neutral. Evaluators of community development programs often question the effectiveness of information programs because many do not result in changes in the behavior of the participants.[2]

Role Conflict and Change. One would expect conflicts to arise between the educator and the community in which he works, between the agency and the community, and between the educator and the agency that employs him. Many observers of community development professionals have noted an interesting progression of role conflicts in community educators.

When a community development professional begins to work in a specific community, he identifies strongly with the sponsoring agency and sees his job as promoting the agency's goals within the community. During this early phase, his chief problem is the community's lack of interest in the agency's goals or lack of trust in the professional himself. The community may dismiss his work as irrelevant to local needs. The professional is unaware of the various leadership structures in the community, does not understand the traditions of the community, and has difficulty gaining access to information. During this first phase, he may feel impotent and alienated. The duration of this phase depends on the skills of the agent, the traditionalism of the community, and the changing external conditions affecting the community.

If the agent is persistent, he gradually gains people's confidence and learns the particular patterns of leadership and resources within the community. He begins to value that particular community and begins to adopt community attitudes and goals as appropriate. As he identifies more closely with the community, he may feel certain of the agency's programs to be inappropriate. Invariably, a conflict grows between the agent and the employing agency. The agency may question whether it is worthwhile to continue its programs in that specific community. If community participation in the agency's programs is low, the agency may fire the agent; if the conflict becomes too strong, the agent may resign.

Agents who survive that second phase enter a third phase in which their identity is neither defined by the agency nor the community. These agents look to both the agency and the community, attempting to develop strategies that maximize the potential of the agency and the pragmatic opportunities in the community. At this stage, many agents feel alienated from both the agency and the community. They can partly remedy this isolation by forming close friendships with other community development professionals who share the same work and problems of loyalty.

Design of Programs

Most theorists of community development, however varied their emphases, describe the goal of development as the growth of interdependence among the individuals and groups in the community. In addition, many stress that the community be encouraged to set common goals and plan activities to meet those goals.

Programming in community development seems to be most effective when based on the following assumptions about individuals, groups, and communities. (1) Each individual in a community has a set of self-interests: economic needs, psychosocial needs, and ideological preferences. (2) Individuals express some of these interests and needs in specific community groups, such as a taxpayers' group formed to advance perceived common economic interests; other interests and needs are distributed over many groups. (3) The community development professional's strategy is to join individuals and groups who have compatible, but not necessarily identical, goals. Successful community development intervention helps disparate groups to see that their individual goals may be met through common activity. (4) This union is achieved through individuals' and groups' recognition of a community problem that they perceive as directly related to their self-interests. (5) As individuals and groups unite to set goals and develop common strategies, the participants in the community development project acquire a sense of their abilities and power to effect change. As changes occur, they feel a sense of accomplishment, and this satisfaction provides motivation for continuing their activities.

The community educator, either professional or volunteer, assists in the process by helping to plan activities that encourage community members to gain knowledge and skills. In public meetings, meetings with small groups, and the taking of surveys, various subgroups within the community can determine common interests. The selection of activities depends on a set of criteria that are derived from the educator's assumptions about individuals and communities. The educator should choose those activities that will help individuals and groups discover their common interests, clarify their common goals and objectives, and develop the skills to realize those goals. Relevant skills include identifying problems, seeking consensus, gathering and analyzing information, setting agenda, eliciting commitments, and self-administration. Throughout, the educator seeks to enhance the growth of the community by helping groups to work more independently and effectively.

In implementing a community development program, the community educator is confronted with an array of problems, such as lethargy, lack of focus, conflict, unresolvable differences of opinion and interest, faulty communication, and a resistance to change.

Lethargy may be defined as the attitude that prevents an individual from recognizing that a problem exists or the attitude that the problem does not concern the individual directly and, therefore, calls for no individual effort. Lethargy acts against individual participation in a community effort. To mitigate lethargic behavior, the educator must help individuals perceive community problems as relevant to their self-interest, to show them how problems in the community prevent them from achieving their personal goals. The educator must also convince individuals that their efforts will be worthwhile, that they can resolve problems by their actions.

Resistance to change is an attitude similar to lethargy. Members of a community often reject educational activities because they feel that their community is satisfactory and that new actions are not needed. In this instance, the community educator must attempt to stimulate the community's awareness of its unresolved problems that require collective action and that can be resolved by collective effort. One cannot initiate a community development activity until the members of the community believe that there is a problem worthy of their effort, which they are capable of solving.

Scatter and conflicting self-interest present similar problems for the community educator. *Scatter* is the perception that one's self-interests are not shared by other community members. Scatter is present within the community to the extent that individuals see no common goals or shared interests. The educator must plan activities that assist individuals to communicate with one another and detect the goals that they have in common. Sometimes individuals have conflicting self-interests; for example, a real estate

developer's interests may be in direct conflict with an environ-
mentalist's goal of preserving open spaces. Increased communication is unlikely to help these two people develop common goals.
Perhaps the only effective strategy for the educator is to help the
individuals to use the community's political process to mediate between their conflicting goals.

Strategies for resolving such problems in community education are predicated on the educator's basic assumptions about
learning and the goals for community development. The strategies
suggested here rest on two basic assumptions about learning. Our
first premise is that adults learn best when the problems they are
studying are important to their own interests. (For support for this
assertion, see Kidd, 1973, and Knowles, 1970.) Second, we assume
that communities will continue to learn if they derive a sense of
accomplishment from their efforts to solve community problems.
(See Davie and others, 1975, and MacKeracher, Davie, and Patterson, 1976.) As with all educational efforts, both the form and the
effectiveness of the activities depend upon the beliefs of the educator and the client about education and learning.[3]

Evaluation of Programs

Evaluation is a judgment, based on consensual criteria and
valid information, about the results, effectiveness, and efficiency of
an educational effort. In planning an evaluation, the educator
must first clarify the reasons for evaluating the program, in order
to justify the costs and time required and to determine which aspects of the program are to be analyzed. He must then decide what
information or data to gather, how to gather that information,
what criteria or measures are to be used to analyze the data, and
who will have access to the data. In designing an evaluation, the
educator should also consider how the results will be used and how
they will affect the program. Will the evaluation improve the program or will the restraints of measurement and design cause the
program to become more rigid? Will the evaluation discourage
educators from planning activities that have important goals if
those goals are difficult to measure?[4]

Although there is a need for the evaluation of educational

programs, and evaluation is often mandatory for programs funded by public sources, evaluation proves particularly difficult for group programs with a community client focus. It is difficult to measure and assess the effects of any group's transactions upon the members of the group. In community learning, the relationship between the work of the group and an individual's effectiveness in community roles is particularly difficult to evaluate. If the goal of these educational programs is the development of the community, then, according to MacKeracher, Davie, and Patterson (1976) there are at least three basic ways to measure development; one can measure changes in resources, changes in problem-solving and decision-making processes, or changes in individual community members' competencies. The educator will, of course, select those measures of development that are appropriate to his program's goals.

The unintended effects that evaluation may have on a program present a special difficulty. An evaluation that measures changes in a community's resources may unfairly emphasize the effective action of one or two individuals who already possess well-developed community skills. In this case, the educational goals of the program are not fairly served by the criteria of the evaluation. An evaluation must use criteria that are congruent with the goals of the educational program.

A final set of problems in the evaluation of programs concerns who should set the criteria, who will collect the data, and who will make the evaluative judgments. A program has at least three potential evaluators: the agency funding the community development program, the community educator or agent, and the individual community members. If their goals are congruent, then a single evaluation may suffice. If their goals are in conflict, then the evaluators will have to collect data for all three sets of criteria.[5]

Adult educators who use community groups as a vehicle for achieving community development encounter difficulties as they attempt to help these groups choose among conflicting goals. In his efforts at consensus building, the adult educator must consider the relative power of various groups and decide whether he will seek to alter the power balances. To achieve community consensus he may play the role of analyst, investigator, community organizer, or community agent, each of which calls for a particular orientation. In many cases, as he becomes intimately involved with the life and values of the groups with which he works he tends to pay less attention to the orientation of his employing organization. His own educational philosophy and his knowledge of adult learning are major influences on the kinds of programs he develops as well as the approaches and emphases he takes in evaluating community development programs.

Comments by the Senior Authors

[1] Adult educators who work in community institutions and agencies need to ask what it means to be an adult educator in these situations. How are the adult educator's contributions specifically educational? How do they differ from a sociologist's or a regional planner's contributions?

[2] If we assume that the adult educator has an educational duty to the community, we may ask which of these roles are appropriate for educators.

[3] We wish to underscore Davie's two assumptions as basic to adult education in the community setting. Adult educators working in a community must not lose sight of these assumptions as they attempt to involve people in community activities.

[4] The increased emphasis on accountability for all adult education agencies and institutions lends urgency to the problems of evaluating the effectiveness of community adult education programs. Clearly, a great deal of research is necessary in this area. Adult educators need evaluative methods that enable them to evaluate and describe a large variety of educational activities.

[5] Davie raises several questions that apply directly to Boyle's discussion of community involvement in planning (see Chapter Seven).

Chapter Ten

◆◆◆◆◆◆◆◆◆◆◆◆◆◆◆◆◆◆◆◆◆◆◆◆
◆◆◆◆◆◆◆◆◆◆◆◆◆◆◆◆◆◆◆◆◆◆◆◆

Community Education for Group Growth

◆◆◆◆◆◆◆◆◆◆◆◆◆◆◆◆◆◆◆◆◆◆◆◆
◆◆◆◆◆◆◆◆◆◆◆◆◆◆◆◆◆◆◆◆◆◆◆◆

M. Donald Campbell

Educators have long recognized the community as a setting for adult education. Although a large number of adult education programs are conducted in the group mode, as Jensen (1964) notes, educators in the twentieth century have introduced formal instruction in natural social settings. Educational activities that occur in such natural settings, outside the traditional classroom, are the subject of this chapter. Our particular focus is the group growth that results from community problem-solving groups. Although this type of educational activity is not the only form of adult education in the community mode, it is especially appropriate for our discussion because of our emphasis on group growth.

First, we will show the educational benefits of establishing community problem-solving groups and describe their activities.

Then we will discuss how such activities can promote group growth and how educators can facilitate such growth.

Educational Value of Community Problem-Solving Groups

For several decades, educators have found community groups a useful mode in adult education. Gruen (1956, p. 86) explains that "the shared experience of a group facing a community problem and searching for knowledge applicable to solution of the problem may, in effect, provide a kind of education for if the problem and the relevant knowledge are made public, it may be, within limits, a very good education indeed." Thelen (1968, p. 29) argues the particular importance of community learning in a democratic society, claiming "there is no place where the citizen role . . . is taught. It probably cannot be taught effectively apart from its proper context of co-operative action. . . . [Community problem-solving groups] can be regarded as a vast adult education program directed to learning of the operational meanings of democracy."

Dewey's philosophy of education suggests the possibility of community education as well. Dewey (1956, p. 117) claims "the primary root of all educational activity is in the instinctive, impulsive attitudes and activities. . . . Numberless spontaneous activities . . . are capable of educational use." An educator, he argues, should begin with the student's spontaneous activity, the nature of this activity is not that important, because he can then guide the student toward more disciplined activity. Community problem-solving groups are similar to these impulsive activities. As a group engages in solving community problems, the educator can develop the potential of that activity, helping the group to define an area in which members desire to grow and enabling the group to organize learning activities that lead to growth.

This mode of adult education has several advantages over other forms of adult education. First, organizing a problem-solving group likely involves less time and energy than organizing a traditional instructional group. A community problem-solving group may organize itself before approaching an adult educator, and its members may be highly motivated to work together. With the group's consent, the educator can then direct this group's motivation to educational ends.

A second advantage is that the subject of the community mode of adult education is directly relevant to the learners' lives. Dewey (1956, p. 14) says a school should be a "genuine form of active community life, instead of a place set apart to learn lessons." He claims that "there should be a natural connection of the everyday life of the child with the business environment about him, and that it is the affair of the school to clarify and liberalize this connection . . . by keeping alive the ordinary bonds of relation" (1956, p. 76). Dewey urges that the materials be "as 'real,' as direct and straightforward, as opportunity permits" (p. 124). Community problem-solving groups require no special effort to maintain this bond between classroom activity and the outside world.

Last, community problem-solving groups address the needs of adults. Unlike children and adolescents who learn to enable themselves to assume their future roles in society, adults are now living their roles and thus shoulder a variety of responsibilities. The problems adults face in their roles offer a prime opportunity for education. Rogers (1969, p. 130) claims that effective education requires that "the individual be in contact with, be faced by, a problem which he perceives as a real problem for him." Community problem-solving groups try to solve such real problems. Educators who are able to develop the educational potential of these groups could promote considerable growth for individuals, groups, and communities.

Community Problem-Solving Activities

A community problem-solving group is a group of citizens who voluntarily attempt to solve a problem in their community. A community is "a concentrated settlement of people in a limited territorial area, within which they satisfy many of their daily needs through a system of interdependent relationships. . . . Community also implies a certain identification of the inhabitants with the geographical area, and with each other, a feeling of sharing common interests and goals, a certain amount of mutual cooperation, and an awareness of the existence of the community in both its inhabitants and those in the surrounding area" (Theodorson and Theodorson, 1969, pp. 63–64). A community's problem may be a social, physical, or economic one. The entire community may or may not view a given situation as a problem.

Community problem-solving groups assume varied forms. A group might organize to work on a specific problem. Such a group may be part of a planned community development activity, or it may emerge spontaneously as a few citizens become aroused about a particular problem. The members of the group might be neighbors concerned about a particular problem or citizens from different neighborhoods. They may not have known one another prior to their participation in the group, yet their common interest in a certain community problem draws them together. Community problem-solving groups may be affiliated with certain community organizations; for example the Rotary, Lions, or Kiwanis service clubs may appoint a community problem-solving committee. A community-wide organization, such as a community council, is another example of a community problem-solving group. Members of this council may include representatives from service clubs, special interest groups, and other organizations in the community and citizens who volunteer to serve on the council irrespective of their affiliation with another community group.

Community problem-solving groups differ from many other voluntary community groups. Groups whose primary concerns are recreation or social activity and support groups designed to help individuals cope with personal problems (alcoholism, divorce, parenthood) focus on the individual or group. Although such groups are composed of community members and they may meet in a community facility, they do not establish communications with the community as part of their normal activity. Such groups fall within the group mode. In contrast, community problem-solving groups operate in the community mode: They attempt to solve community problems, rather than individual problems, and they have access to the community during their problem-solving activity. For instance, group members may consult with various professionals, who are not in the group, and local government officials. The group also comes in contact with the community when it attempts to implement its solution to the community problem.

Some might argue, however, that a community problem-solving group is not concerned with the welfare of the entire community, but rather with its own special interest. The activities of an elected or appointed governmental body, they might argue, are more likely to benefit the community as a whole. Indeed, many citizens choose to participate in formal civic activities. They run for mayor, serve on a zoning committee, seek employment with the public works department, or attend city council meetings and public hearings to offer their opinions on a certain issue. Public political activity, however, is only one form of community activity. Because communities are not necessarily coextensive with legal, political, or governmental units, their problems cannot always be addressed by an established municipal body. For example, in urban areas, residents may define their community and its problems at the level of neighborhoods; in rural areas, however, farmers living in several townships might compose a community.

Because the boundaries of a community are not necessarily equivalent to those of local government, community activity includes more than public activity. Government officials are not the only people who can identify the interests of a certain area and co-operate to solve problems. Private citizens can as well. Voluntary community problem-solving groups, then, are forms of community activity that address community problems. Although only a small group of people may define a given situation in the community as a problem, the community as a whole may benefit from this group's problem-solving activity. Granted, the group's proposed solution will likely benefit its members. Such personal benefit motivates these citizens to work on the problem. But such benefits are not necessarily incongruent with the public interest.

Campbell (1977) provides two examples that support this argument. A group of citizens who lived outside the boundaries of the nearby village had no municipal sewage service; each landowner had his own septic system. Over the years, several septic systems malfunctioned and the waste seeped into a nearby lake. Although county zoning ordinances required septic tanks to be away from the lake, many homeowners, whose homes had been built on small lots before the zoning ordinances existed, could not comply with these regulations. One woman, whose septic system had recently malfunctioned, organized a group to take action. While having her system repaired, she realized the importance of adequate sewage facilities and she learned that the county zoning administrator could initiate legal action against a homeowner whose septic system did not comply with zoning regulations. The community group established a sanitary district as a first step toward obtaining municipal sewer service. Although protecting their property values may have been the primary motivation of these citizens, their actions benefited the community as well. Installation of a municipal sewage system would halt the deterioration of the lake so that people could continue to use it for recreational purposes. By establishing a sanitary district, the citizens' group also helped the town board because a sanitary district can apply for federal funds on low-interest loans.

Citizens of another group that benefited their community lived near a wintering spot for bald eagles. They discovered that the tract of land where the eagles roosted was for sale. The owner, unaware that eagles roosted on his property, intended to sell to the highest bidder. If a commercial developer bought the land, the eagles' survival would be jeopardized. After some time, this citizens' group secured enough money to buy the land and establish an eagle refuge. These citizens valued wildlife preservation and wanted to protect the eagles. Although not all citizens shared their personal concern, the majority of the community did.

In the two examples cited, the community supported the problem-solving group's activities. Sometimes, of course, a particular group's actions or proposed solutions conflict with the desires of other community groups. These other groups may not benefit from the initiating group's solution to a certain community problem. An urban businessmen's group, for example, may wish to improve the community in ways quite different from those that a group of farmers might desire. Both groups are motivated by their own special interests: Businessmen want to boost the local economy and farmers seek to preserve their farmland. Both groups may believe they have the community's best interest in mind. Yet, motivated by their special interests, the group's respective solutions benefit only a certain segment of the community, not the community as a whole.

Thelen (1968) discusses such conflicts, observing that "individuals are concerned about different aspects of the culture; and that the individuals with similar concerns tend to affiliate with each other and become a 'group'. As a group, they state their purposes by differentiating out of the community culture as a whole certain particular objects which best represent their concerns. . . . Thus many a 'community organization' ends up only with people from the same class level" (p. 341). "Under these typical conditions, the organization is likely to have its own class view of community problems and to arrive at poor, or at least partial, solutions, because the problem was never really seen realistically as a whole" (p. 345). Thus, the two groups disagree because each has a limited view of what is good for the community as a whole.

Such a situation offers a prime opportunity for growth because each group can broaden its narrow view. As Biddle and Biddle (1965, p. 116) note, "some enthusiasts for a special interest can be persuaded to broaden their objectives. They move toward a concept of all-inclusive community." In the process of developing this more inclusive view of the community, the group will grow. Before discussing how education can foster such growth, we shall consider the meaning of group growth.

Group Growth

Dewey (1916) defines growth as the development of "active capacities to readjust activity to meet new conditions" (p. 52) and the "constant expansion of horizons and consequent formation of new purposes, new responses" (p. 175). Growth involves the accumulation of learning: "in learning one act, methods are developed [that are] good for use in other situations" (1961, p. 45). Earlier experiences prepare us for "a later experience of a deeper and more expansive quality" (1916, p. 47). Dewey's description of individual growth can be applied to groups as well. Assuming, as Bion (1959, p. 133) does, that a "group is more than the sum of its members," one can refer to the group as a whole. Granted, individual members compose a group, and without them the group would not exist. Yet a group's members interact in ways that are determined by the group as an entity. (For a discussion of the group as an entity, see Chapter Four.)

Like individuals, groups can develop their capacities to respond to new situations. For example, a group that resolves a minor disagreement between two members has thereby improved its ability to handle conflict. That group may later draw on this acquired skill when attempting to resolve a more complex conflict. More effort and new strategy will likely be necessary, but the group develops its strategy based on its previous experiences with conflict. All successful resolutions of conflict reflect the group's growth in this area.

Dewey (1938, p. 79) suggests that growth "depends on the presence of a difficulty to be overcome. What is necessary is to arouse the individual to engage in an active quest for information and the production of new ideas and facts. This then becomes the ground for further experiences in which new problems are presented." In the example of the group that faced internal dissension, the process of overcoming this difficulty occasioned the group's growth. In community problem-solving groups, the difficulties to be overcome are the various problems the community group faces.

Overcoming difficulties and solving problems promote growth only when the succeeding problems are more complex than preceding ones. Otherwise the group will merely use skills and abilities previously developed and will fail to develop new ones. Biddle and Biddle (1965, p. 61) note that the "satisfaction and self-confidence gained from small accomplishments can lead to the contending with more and more difficult problems, in a process of continuing growth." Thus, we define group growth as the development of abilities to solve problems of increasing complexity.

The two community problem-solving groups described earlier show signs of sustaining their growth. The group that established the sanitary district is working to construct a municipal sewer system, a more complex task. The group will rely on the abilities it has already developed and will need to develop new ones. The group that established the eagle refuge is considering two new projects: the purchase of additional land for wildlife preservation and the formulation of a county land use plan. Proposing a land use policy is more complex than buying a piece of land. To establish a general plan for land use, the group will have to work closely with a large number of community and official groups.

Solving this problem will, thus, require the group to develop new skills and talents.

Unfortunately, however, not all community problem-solving groups grow. Groups may begin well but fail to continue because of conflict within the group or pressure from the community. Some groups do not build on their success or progress, but retreat from further action. As a result, these groups' skills atrophy. Educators, however, who recognize the potential for a group's regression, can play an important role in community problem-solving groups, as we now will describe.

The Educator's Contribution to Group Growth

Community problem-solving activity has the potential to be educational, but it is not synonymous with education. Education comprises "those organized and planned activities in which man engages for the purpose of learning something" ("What Is Adult Education? . . . ," 1955, p. 134). An adult may learn from a variety of experiences or activities, including community problem-solving activity. Only those experiences or activities, however, which are organized to facilitate learning in a planned manner fall within the domain of education. (For additional arguments in favor of this distinction, see "What Is Adult Education? . . . ," 1955.) Biddle and Biddle (1965, p. viii), in contrast, equate action with education, arguing that "because it develops human beings, community development is an educational enterprise." This argument, however, focuses too strongly on the results of community activity. Unplanned, or incidental, growth may result from a number of activities that were not planned as educational experiences. For instance, a group may grow as it attempts to solve a community problem. As Jensen (1964, p. 107) notes, this growth "is not a consciously directed affair but rather the result of spontaneous participation in the day-to-day activities of the society." Such growth, incidental to work on the problem the group has identified, is an example of incidental change. The extent of this incidental growth varies from group to group.[1]

Educators can facilitate growth in community problem-solving groups. For example, an adult educator working with a group might note that the group is experiencing difficulties in communicating. This educator could promote the group's growth by helping the members to plan a way to resolve their communication problems. The group could temporarily put aside work on the community problem and take time to examine its communication patterns. The adult educator, or some other consultant, might conduct a short workshop on the topic. Planned educational activities can facilitate growth more effectively than a group's efforts by trial and error.

A group's need for effective leadership offers another opportunity for adult educators. A community problem-solving group may eventually discover, by trial and error, the most effective kind of leadership for a given community problem, or a member who has worked in other groups may suggest the kind of leadership the group needs. Groups whose members have little experience in group activity may gropingly fail to discover an effective style of leadership. Poor leadership prevents a group from resolving certain other difficulties and, when a lack of progress is apparent, members often quit. An adult educator can help a group to plan activities that will develop the group's abilities to resolve this problem. Workshops or individual leadership training tutorials would be appropriate.

Adult educators may help a community problem-solving group grow in other areas as well. Thelen (1968) discusses several internal problems that a group must solve. A group must help its members feel a part of the group. A group also needs to develop a balance of emotion, rational thought, and action. Some groups devote so much time to discussion of strategy that they fail to take action. Other groups freely express emotions but do not engage in reflective thought. Groups have to acquire skills to evaluate their achievement and resolve problems in their process, including the ability to make decisions in an open, rational manner. As a group resolves these internal difficulties, the group experiences growth.

Thelen (1968) also discusses groups' external problems, their relationships with other community groups. Groups must learn to co-operate with other sectors of the community: local government officials, special interest groups, and the like. Groups must be able to relate to both those who favor their position and those who oppose it. Again, educators can help community problem-solving groups learn and grow.

Thus far, we have discussed only the growth of a community problem-solving group. But this group is not the only group that can grow from community problem-solving activity. Its efforts may stimulate incidental growth in other community groups as well. Biddle and Biddle (1965) suggest that a group's activity sets an example that may arouse other groups to action. One neighborhood group's success with a particular community problem may encourage citizens in other neighborhoods to form new groups to work on similar problems. A neighborhood group's growth may also influence existing community organizations to renew their activity. Some of these organizations may have been formed to resolve the problem on which the neighborhood group is working. Over the years, however, they may have become less sensitive to community problems and less active. Action by a neighborhood group may provoke these organizations to grow responsive once again to needs in the community.

Some community problem-solving groups are coalitions of representatives of various community groups. As the members of the coalition work together on their project, they can incidentally share concerns about their own groups. Although this sharing may not be part of the coalition's official agenda, such informal exchanges can stimulate growth in the community groups involved. Coalition members can discuss problems their groups are having and benefit from other members' experience and suggestions.

The activities of a problem-solving group may, in addition to encouraging others' incidental growth, facilitate planned educational growth. A coalition may attempt to promote cooperation among its constituent groups by planning discussions, workshops, and lectures. A consulting adult educator could help the coalition plan such activities. A community problem-solving group can also encourage growth by organizing new groups. Each member of the coalition might agree to organize a neighborhood group to work on the problem. Organizing these groups presents certain difficulties that require the coalition to develop new skills. Coalition members may need to learn how to recruit people for their group, how to organize their group's activities, and what educational materials to use. An adult educator who is working with the coalition can meet with the group to discuss ways to solve these problems. He might also offer leadership training for those members who will be forming neighborhood groups. As a result of this educational activity, new groups will be established and the coalition will learn new skills. The individuals and groups involved will experience growth in their abilities to resolve their community's problems.

Finally, growth may result from conflicts among the desires of different community problem-solving groups. For example, two groups may have opposing views on how to improve their community. Thelen (1968) suggests that these groups plan a joint project, either a compromise between their initially conflicting ideas or an entirely new project. As these two groups work together, they, in effect, form a third group. As this third group grows, the two original groups may grow as well. By working together, the groups develop their abilities to co-operate with others. The decision-making and leadership skills that the third group acquires may benefit the two original groups.

Sometimes opposing groups meet together on their own initiative to work through their problems. Often, however, such groups continue to fight one another and do not learn to cooperate. An adult educator can initiate meetings with the two opposing groups. With the consent of both groups, he can, for example, try to explain one group's position to the other. He might note areas of agreement between the groups and areas in which the groups apparently misunderstand one another's position. The educator's analysis can aid the groups' growth in understanding and cooperating with one another.

How should an adult educator work with community problem-solving groups? First, he must realize he is primarily an educator, not an agent for social change, a consultant, a local developer, a social planner, or a community organizer. Literature that describes the educator as the agent of social change considers education as a means for social change (see Alinsky, 1971; Gallaher and Santopolo, 1967; Lippitt, 1959; Rothman, 1974). Education, however, must be the primary end for an educator; the process of working toward social change is a means to this end.

The educator wants the group to successfully resolve the

community problem they have identified and he offers them whatever information and training he can. But, in contrast to a social planner or a community organizer, he must always look for ways to plan educational activities that will promote the group's growth. Although a group may fail to solve a community problem, it may grow during the experience such that it will be more successful in problem-solving activity at a later time.

A primary difficulty that faces the educator is that the group will grow overly dependent on him. An educator working with a group may so want the group to succeed that he does much of the work himself. Although the educator's work may solve the community's problem, the group may not have grown in the process, since it depended on the educator to do the work. Just as a student does not develop competence if he relies too heavily on his teacher, if a problem-solving group does not work out at least some of the problems without the educator's help, the group will not have learned how to solve community problems. A group that is too dependent on the educator will not know how to proceed in the future. Members' frustration may then be so threatening to the group that it regresses and terminates all activity.

Franklin (1969) lists five different styles of working with community groups, the first four of which, he claims, foster the group's dependence on the educator. The *instructor* concentrates on transmitting information to the group. The *paterfamilias* relates to the group as a father figure, often attempting to protect the group from conflict. The *advocate* has decided what the group should do and urges it to adopt his ideas. And the *servitor* merely accomplishes what the group wishes. The fifth style, that of the *community change educator,* does not encourage dependency. This educator, Franklin states, helps adults "learn the how and why of change and development. He takes initiative in generating a learning environment for change. . . . He helps delineate what the client needs to know throughout the process and helps the client obtain such knowledge and skill from available sources, including himself (p. 9). Franklin also affirms the priority of the learners' growth; the educator "is aware of the client system's process of development. He remains as sensitive to the organic life of the group as to its chosen target" (p. 17).

How is an educator to establish a productive relationship with a community problem-solving group? This question merits research. Campbell (1977) sought to determine ways that an adult educator working with these groups can encourage group growth. He suggests three different educational styles. The first is the educator as a provider of information. The educator offers the group information relevant to the community problem. For instance, he might share his knowledge of state statutes that affect the group's plans. The group learns as it analyzes this new information. (McClusky, 1973, describes this approach in more detail.) Although this style is similar to Franklin's instructor, its use need not encourage dependency on the educator. Judicious provision of information can be an effective stimulus to a group's growth.

A second style is that of the demonstrator: the educator demonstrates some action the first time, so that the group can later take similar actions. For example, the educator might assume extensive responsibility for the group's first community problem-solving effort, such that the group can assume primary responsibility for future efforts. (This approach is discussed further by Abshier, 1973.) To use this style most effectively, the educator must involve the group members in his activities and offer reasons for his actions. Biddle and Biddle (1965) support the demonstrator style, suggesting that the educator assume an active role early in the problem-solving effort and reduce his involvement later.

In contrast to the demonstrator, the facilitator, the third style, puts primary responsibility on the group from the beginning. Using a variety of strategies, he introduces educational activity whenever the group has difficulty. Several of these strategies are described by Franklin (1969) and Biddle and Biddle (1965).[2]

These broad styles suggest various ways that an adult educator can work with a community problem-solving group. An educator's particular work with a group always reflects personal, social, and cultural factors. Obviously the educator's personality influences his work. An aggressive extrovert will surge ahead to organize educational workshops, while a more introverted educator will operate more slowly and more informally. An educator's personal style will determine, in part, the kind of growth his group experiences.

The social system influences an educator's work with a group as well. Each group is unique in certain respects and thus requires specific kinds of assistance. A group that suffers from ineffective leadership may need a highly organized workshop on leadership, while a group that has difficulty communicating may resist an educator's attempts to conduct a workshop on communication, preferring a less formal process of education. As a group's needs and competencies change, the educator will need to adjust his educational style.

Finally, each community is different, and the educator will be influenced by the community's style. One community may encourage citizen activity, whereas another may discourage it. In some communities, citizen groups continually oppose one another's efforts; other communities have very apathetic citizens. The adult educator must develop educational strategies appropriate to encourage group growth in each kind of community.

Comments by the Senior Authors

[1] Campbell delineates the unique contribution that the adult educator can make in the community setting. The educator is responsible for the organizing and planning of experiences and activities designed to facilitate learning. Although Campbell acknowledges that considerable unplanned learning takes place, he argues that the adult educator's primary responsibility concerns planned learning.

[2] The reader may wish to compare Campbell's statement of the adult educator's role with those proposed by Boyle (Chapter Seven) and Davie (Chapter Nine). The similarities and differences obviously point to different emphases and value systems. What consequences do these different positions have for adult education? Our choice among these positions determines, in large part, the direction of our practice.

Chapter Eleven

◆◆◆◆◆◆◆◆◆◆◆◆◆◆◆◆◆◆◆◆◆◆
◆◆◆◆◆◆◆◆◆◆◆◆◆◆◆◆◆◆◆◆◆

Individual Growth Through Community Problem Solving

◆◆◆◆◆◆◆◆◆◆◆◆◆◆◆◆◆◆◆◆◆◆
◆◆◆◆◆◆◆◆◆◆◆◆◆◆◆◆◆◆◆◆◆

Chere C. Coggins

"Humankind will survive only through the commitment and involvement of individuals in their own and others' growth and development as human beings" (Kubler-Ross, 1975, Preface). No longer willing to sit back and have their lives directed by others, people all over the United States are actively attempting to resolve the problems that confront them. We find a rural community searching for ways to attract and maintain doctors and paramedical personnel. A rising level of juvenile delinquency prompts another community group to establish a downtown drop-in center for youth. A third community group directs its attention toward improving local housing. What are the results of such community problem-solving efforts? What effects do these efforts have on the lives of individuals, the problem-solving group itself, and the community? What are the implications of such activities for adult education?

Let us consider the example of community development in such fields as agricultural economics and rural sociology. Although these programs were designed to increase the gross national product, create new jobs, and provide new or improved hospitals or recreational facilities, we can inquire about their educational success. If we define educative growth in Dewey's (1916, p. 54) terms as the "constant expansion of new horizons and the consequent formation of new purposes, new responses . . . the cumulative movement of action toward a later result," it would appear that community problem-solving efforts provide the potential for growth of this type. But it seems that we, as adult educators, have not sufficiently reflected on these community problem-solving activities, on the quality and nature of the educative growth they can occasion.[1]

Biddle and Biddle (1965), Campbell (1976), Coggins (1976), Franklin and Franklin (1976), and Thelen (1968) have given us some insights into the educative growth effected by community problem solving. Individuals learn facts about their community and about specific problems. They also develop skills that enable them to participate in groups and solve problems. Problem-solving groups learn to cooperate with other problem-solving groups to discuss concerns that touch both groups; groups develop techniques for managing their internal conflicts. Communities that were once apathetic develop a community spirit of self-help, learn the importance of co-operation, and discover their community's identity through self-understanding. Growth incidental to the problem-solving activities, as well as planned growth may result from community learning. Educative growth can occur in individuals, including the adult educator, the problem-solving group, and the community as a result of their involvement in community problem-solving activities. Let us first direct our attention to the individual's growth.

Individual Growth

There are several types of individual involvement in community problem-solving processes. We have individuals who are integrally involved in the community problem-solving group and its activities; we have those individuals who could be considered the target population; and a third group of individuals who may be affected incidentally. For example, consider a community struck by Dutch elm disease. Soil erosion is severe, havens for wildlife disappear, and the beauty of the community is ravaged. Through community meetings, the community decides to form a problem-solving group that will help individuals in the community solve the problem that faces the entire community. Their educational effort takes many forms. Individuals are notified of the availability of pamphlets, journals, books, and short independent study courses on topics such as the varieties of indigenous trees, growth rates of various plants and shrubs, and prevention of soil erosion. Self-directed individual learning is encouraged. Panels of experts speak at meetings, formal classes and group tours are organized—all efforts to help individuals understand the cause of the problem, its immediate and enduring consequences, and the actions necessary to resolve this community problem.

Although adult educators traditionally have evaluated the educative effect of self-study units, we have not adequately assessed the educative results of community problem-solving activities. Nor have we given sufficient consideration to those people who chose not to avail themselves of community educational offerings.

Research in the fields of human development, education, psychology, and educational psychology provides us with many insights into the general concept of individual growth. We find an emphasis on growth as a process rather than a product. Dewey (1938) notes that growth should not be regarded as having an end, but rather as being an end. Maslow (1962) describes growth as the progression of higher and higher levels of psychological needs, and Fromm (1968, p. 12) emphasizes growth as a movement "towards becoming more human, more humane" in his depiction of the progressive, dynamic nature of growth. Frankl's (1959) discussion of man's search for meaning suggests that it is our very humanness that causes the individual to continue to grow. Or, as May (1953, p. 93) states "every organism has one and only one central need in life, to fulfill its own potentialities . . . [yet] his development is never automatic, but must be to some extent chosen and affirmed by himself." Thus, individuals have an innate capacity and need to grow, and their growth is self-directed.

Several authors suggest that in addition to our need for physical survival we have "transurvival" needs that we fulfill by "free and spontaneous activities expressing man's facilities and seeking meaning beyond utilitarian work" (Fromm, 1968, p. 42). Maslow (1962) posits a closely parallel conceptualization. He theorizes that there are basic needs—those of air, water, food, shelter, safety—and "meta-needs" or growth needs, such as love, belongingness, and self-esteem. The thought processes and actions that help us fulfill the latter needs constitute growth.

In discussing conditions necessary for growth, Dewey (1916, p. 52) assumes that "Power to grow depends on a need for others and plasticity. Plasticity, or the power to learn from experience, means the formation of new habits. Habits take the form of both habituation or a general and persistent balance of organic activities with the surroundings and of active capacities to readjust to new conditions. The former furnishes the background for growth, the latter constitutes growing." This growth, however, "depends on the presence of a difficulty to be overcome by the exercise of intelligence" (p. 79).

What specific aspects of individual growth may be enhanced through involvement in community problem-solving processes? The literature of adult education, community development, and community problem solving speaks of the potential for educative growth in this context. Community development is described as a "process of enrichment and qualitative growth" (Poston, 1954, p. 193) and as the "instructional management of that kind of interaction between the community . . . and its people which leads to the development of both" (McClusky, 1960, p. 419). Although community development was hailed as a "new program area in adult education" in the 1960s (Knowles, 1970), researchers have largely ignored the educational results of community programs, preferring to study the field's philosophies and assumptions (Biddle and Biddle, 1965) and its processes and strategies (Cary, 1970; Littrell, 1970; Long, Anderson, and Blubaugh, 1973).

Among the few analyses of individual growth, we have Biddle and Biddle's (1965) discussion of how participation in community problem-solving activities can improve the individual's democratic skills, his sense of responsibility to serve the common good and his understanding of the common good, his ethical sensitivity and willingness to cooperate. Noting the growing need for accountability, Wileden (1970) stresses the importance of evaluating personal growth, development of group skills, and changes in attitudes and views. Thelen (1968), Franklin and Franklin (1976), and other researchers touch on various aspects of individual growth as they recount case histories of community problem-solving groups.

Although the literature provides us with individual growth in many areas and with different emphases, research has been fragmentary and it lacks a unified theoretical framework. If we, as adult educators, are to enhance educative growth in community problem-solving transactions, we must have a clear understanding of the types of individual growth that community problem-solving activities can promote. The following schema is based on research employing grounded theory methodology, as elaborated by Glaser and Strauss (1967). Our analysis of the literature, both case studies and conceptual work, was compared with data obtained from interviews and participant-observation of members involved in community problem-solving groups. This comparison yielded a number of categories, properties, and indicators that define individual growth resulting from community problem-solving activities.

We have identified four categories of individual growth: growth related to one's self; growth related to interactions with others; growth related to life; and growth pertaining to the areas of knowledge and process. We selected the term, *stance* to connote the individual's position in each domain of growth. *Stance* encompasses more than the individual's attitude; it connotes the individual's cognitive, affective, and psychomotor position. Other researchers have used the term *orientation,* which we accept as equivalent to *stance.*

Stance Toward Self. We asked people who had participated in community problem-solving activities to describe how they had changed as a result of their involvement. One commented, "I'm a pusher. I'm always disappointed that people can't move as fast as I would like to have them. This was pointed out to me." Another answered, "I felt so dumb when I first attended these meetings, and after a while you find out that the expert didn't know all the answers either." These comments and others suggest that one aspect of a changing stance toward self is the growth of self-awareness.

The second property related to an individual's stance toward self that we detected is one's sense of personal worth. A seventy-year-old man, relating his experiences in a community problem-solving group five years earlier said, with pride and misty eyes, "I have been here a long time and I knew a lot of people and they knew me . . . and somehow they [the community problem-solving group that approached him to work with them] thought I could do some good." At age sixty-five, he proudly took an active part in community problem-solving processes for the first time in his life, and he continued to do so at age seventy. Others look back with pride at certain stands they took, at personal risks they assumed. Regression, the antithesis of growth, also seems evident. One individual announced bitterly, "My ideas were squelched." Sadly enough, he did not understand why his suggestions were ignored, only that no one cared for his ideas.

Self-development is a third aspect of one's stance toward self. Both the literature and our interviewees speak to this innate concern on the part of individuals, albeit stifled from time to time by forces such as inactivity and passivity. We spoke with a minister who was involved in a community problem-solving group that was having difficulties in communicating. He joined a transactional analysis group (TA), noting the ensuing difficulties in his problem-solving group as one of the major reasons he chose TA. This new pursuit would, he hoped, aid his personal development.

From the insights and indicators we found in the literature and our field data, we identify three properties of individual growth related to stance toward self as self-awareness, self-worth, and self-development. Through experiences in the community mode, individuals can learn more about who they are, can learn to value what they are, and can develop new skills and attitudes.

Stance Toward Others. Although the literature provides few indicators of individual growth as related to others, our interview data indicate that involvement in community problem-solving activities provides an excellent opportunity for individuals to learn not only from one another but also about one another. Persons spoke of discovering strengths in others that they had not realized before. For example, one individual noted, "I would say there were a lot of people who showed signs of leadership among those who were involved . . . that I would not have identified that way." Another commented on his surprise at the depth of support and commitment of the community. An urban dweller in a rural area reflected on the implications of an enhanced understanding between individuals, groups, and communities in conflict. He felt that, as a result of urban and rural groups having worked together in a community problem-solving group, "there are few farmers I can't sit down with and talk with now." This example, which might appear to be merely one individual's growth, illustrates the permanent effects that problem solving can have on community relations.

Individuals discover, however, not only the strengths of others but also their weaknesses. Although the discovery of weaknesses represents growth in the understanding of others, this enhanced understanding can result in regression. For example, an individual who realized that his group could not accommodate individuals with somewhat dissimilar needs and interests commented, "It's more than you can take after awhile and you feel all alone, nobody that you can confide in." Unable to understand the group's failure to resolve the conflict, he felt alienated and he withdrew from the community.

Many participants in the problem-solving groups described their increased appreciation of the contributions of others: "I'm a better man having met Father R. and worked together with him. I have a lot of respect for him. I think I have gained myself, through interacting with him." We see indications of appreciation of individuals not only for what they can offer, but also for who they are. One woman involved in the resettlement of a Vietnamese refugee family, a community project, noted, "I think about them, the Vietnamese, with a very good feeling." Another, discussing her relationship with a Vietnamese family, and one particular young girl in the family, said, "And I loved her." These comments express the closeness, love, and respect that can grow between two individuals brought together through community problem-solving activities.

In tandem with the appreciation of others is the individual's growing concern for others, what Fromm (1968) calls the development of humanistic conscience. For example, a woman who described herself as "just not the volunteer type" became involved in a project at her pastor's request. When a second, related problem-solving effort was organized, she volunteered her help. When asked why, she said, "You always think, let someone else do it, and nobody else was coming forth and so I felt, in a way, maybe I can do something."

A final aspect of the individual's stance toward others consists of his orientation toward interdependence. One of our interviewees remarked, "I learned to see the beauty of being able to work with other people." Another stated, "I learned if a group of individuals really get together and co-operate, they can do almost anything." Community problem-solving activities can facilitate the individual's understanding of the power and promise of interdependence.

Stance Toward Life. The literature offers many discussions of growth related to a changed understanding of and attitude toward life. Allport (1955) and Rogers (1961) speak of a growing person as one who becomes more active, open, interested, and directed toward the future. Fromm (1968) and Freire (1971) note the importance of the development of faith in oneself, hope for the future, and the courage and willingness to risk failure. Does community problem solving further individuals' openness to the world around them? Does it encourage and enhance a person's desire to become more active, more involved? One man noted that through his involvement in a community problem-solving group he "discovered that there was more to life than sitting in front of the television." Others have, as a result of one community project, become actively involved in community affairs, although they had not been active previously. Thus one aspect of growth in the individual's stance toward life is depth of involvement.

Several researchers have defined a growing person as one who develops an orientation toward the future, yet there is little direct evidence that individuals develop this orientation as a result of involvement in community problem-solving groups. In any group or community of individuals, there are those who look ahead and prepare for the future, rather than simply fighting crises in the present, and those who do not.

Several individuals commented on people's orientation to the future. One indicated that individuals do not want changes in the status quo and thus fail to look for areas in which changes are needed. Another noted, "Unless we realistically look at our reality in the present, it is almost impossible to determine our future needs." Several individuals did note, in retrospect, that they wished they had looked further into the future. As one person suggested, "If we had had the foresight to go ahead with the project when it was first suggested, we would have the system now." This statement tentatively posits a need for orientation to the future.

Community problem solving can arouse individuals' fears of the unknown. One man commented, "I'm very skeptical of starting a new adventure like this. It is very nerve-racking because of so much uncertainty all the way through. We had so many doubts because it was entirely new, and if one thing went wrong . . ." Yet he later noted that if the problem were great he knew he would join another problem-solving group. Many respondents expressed similar feelings. Most were uncertain whether they could accomplish the goal decided upon, but all attempted to forge ahead. Many are amazed, in retrospect, that they did continue when success was so uncertain. We do not know what caused this development of courage and loss of fear of failure. One individual attributed his newly found courage to the "group mind" that seemed to indicate they would succeed even though individual group members were skeptical. This courage to risk failure may be attributable to newly found hope, faith, or a sense of power. Though we are uncertain of its origin, this growth is evident.

Stance Toward Knowledge and Process. Considerable research treats the individual's acquisition of problem-solving skills through actual involvement in solving community problems. (See, in particular, Bennett and Nelson, 1975; Maier, 1963.) Similarly, our interviews yielded plentiful and enlightening evidence. One participant noted, "Most of what I learned, I learned through disillusionment. You begin with illusions, and as they're tested you're relieved of illusions, and you get a better understanding of reality." When we asked people what they would do differently next time, their answers indicated that they had learned from their experience and their disillusionment.

Many persons reflected on the delegation of responsibility within their group. One person noted, "Henry was so involved trying to cover the whole package that it would have been to our benefit to say, 'Oh, I'll take number one, who's going to take number two?'" Similarly, another said, "I learned that if we did something like this again, ecumenically, I think I would be a little more insistent from the beginning to have everything spelled out, who would be responsible for what and where. Try to structure it a little more keenly. I think we left too much to chance." And, indeed, these individuals did just that when working on their second community problem-solving effort.

Others had learned about the allocation of resources and the value of consultation with professionals. Many felt they learned how to communicate with others to resolve conflicts and problems. For example, one person stated, "One of the things I learned through this was to call on people personally. You may have to call on each individual, sit, talk, and answer questions." Many persons agreed the problem-solving process was educational, but only for those who were directly involved.

Almost without exception, people expressed an interest in participating in new community problem-solving activities. Many continued to be involved in on-going groups, finding that helping people and their community was a rewarding, personally satisfying experience. They appreciated the feeling of accomplishment and the fellowship they experienced. Individuals who discover the benefits and beauty of the community problem-solving process affirm this new attitude in continual involvement in these activities. Appreciation of problem-solving activities is another property of an individual's growth related to stance toward knowledge and process.

Participants acquire a range of other knowledge as a result of their involvement in a community problem-solving group. They learn about their community, their local government, and the legislative process, in addition to whatever information they gather about a particular problem.

Schema of Individual Growth. As we have seen, individuals grow in a number of ways as a result of their involvement in community problem-solving groups and activities. As one group member noted, "You can always learn from talking to others. You can learn something from anyone, no matter who he is. He knows something you don't." The evidence seems to bear him out. When people come together to work on community problems, individual growth on the part of the group's members results. We offer the following schema to summarize the types of educative growth we have identified:

> Stance toward self
> > Self-awareness
> > Self-worth
> > Concern for self-development
>
> Stance toward others
> > Understanding of others
> > Appreciation of others
> > Concern for others
> > Interdependence
>
> Stance toward life
> > Depth of involvement
> > Orientation toward the future
> > Courage to risk failure
>
> Stance toward knowledge and process
> > Knowledge of problem-solving processes
> > Appreciation of problem-solving processes
> > Other knowledge

Although community problem-solving activities can facilitate the individual's growth in each of these categories, the potential for regression, the antithesis of growth, is also present. An individual may grow, regress, or remain unchanged in any of these areas.

Enhancing Individual Growth

In order to enhance individuals' growth, adult educators must better understand the relationships among the four categories of individual growth that we have identified. Is one prerequisite to any other? Does growth occur in each simultaneously?

Several theorists have argued that an orientation toward active involvement and a willingness to take risks are prerequisite to growth. Dewey (1938, p. 54) states that intellectual growth is "impossible without an active disposition to welcome points of view hitherto alien, an active desire to entertain considerations which might modify existing purposes. Retention of capacity to grow is the reward of such intellectual hospitality." Allport (1955, p. 66) reasons that "it is only through risk taking and variation that growth can occur." If Dewey and Allport are correct, then an individual's growth in his stance toward life is necessary for growth in any of the other categories.

Once an individual has an open, active, involved stance toward life, either as a result of previous experience or as a direct result of participation in community problem-solving activities, several avenues of further growth are open to him. A developing stance toward life could directly affect his stance toward knowledge and process or his stance toward self, or indirectly affect his stance toward others. The active, involved individual can improve his knowledge and skills through community problem-solving activities because he is open to the new experiences, information, attitudes, and values that he encounters. Similarly, the individual who is open to the world around him and has the courage to look ahead and to be involved will lead a life conducive to self-examination. He will begin to question his strengths and weaknesses, examine his feelings about himself, his attitudes, values, and beliefs. He will define areas for self-development and will grow to better understand and accept himself. Thus, growth in one's stance toward life can directly facilitate one's growth in one's stance toward knowledge and process and stance toward self.

An indirect outcome of one's growth in one's stance toward life seems to be growth in one's stance toward others. As Rogers (1969, p. 96) notes, "When a person accepts himself, he is much more free to hear, understand, and come close to the other. So we find more understanding and closer relationships . . . growing out of this self-acceptance."

Are there relationships between one's stance toward knowledge and process and one's stance toward self or one's stance toward others? Although stance toward knowledge and process does not seem prerequisite to other growth, it does bear some relationship to growth. As individuals acquire new knowledge and skills, they may come to better understand themselves and others. An individual who studies Oriental culture, for example, will better understand visitors from Vietnam and other cultures as well; he will develop an appreciation of cultural differences and similarities. Thus one's stance toward knowledge and process appears to be a vehicle, but not a prerequisite, for growth in other categories.

An adult educator who seeks to maximize individual growth as a desirable outcome of community problem solving must consider the reciprocal relationships among stance toward knowledge and process, stance toward self, and stance toward others because of their complementary influences on the development of an enhanced stance toward life. We could raise similar questions regarding the relationships among properties within the categories. For example, does one have to grow in self-awareness before one experiences changes in one's sense of self-worth? Is a concern for self-development always a direct outcome of growth in self-awareness and self-worth? Does one's growing understanding of interdependence affect one's appreciation of and concern for others? Is a growing courage to risk failure prerequisite to a greater depth of involvement in life? These are the kind of questions that emerge as we attempt to analyze individual growth.[2]

Our analysis, furthermore, must consider not only individual growth in the context of community problem solving but also the influence of the problem-solving activity on individual growth. We must identify the factors that operate in a problem-solving group which define the parameters of individual growth for that group's members. Clearly, one set of factors that influences the members' growth is the nature of the problem-solving processes operating within the group. These processes are, in turn, determined by the nature of the persons in the group, their levels of expertise, and their norms and expectations. If we agree with Dewey (1938, p. 79) that "growth depends on the presence of a difficulty to be overcome by the exercise of intelligence," then individuals must have a problem to solve and the opportunity to exercise their intelligence to solve the problem. This opportunity is presented by the problem-solving process.

Community problem-solving processes assume a variety of forms. The process of a given problem-solving activity depends on the number of people involved, their abilities to act independently and interdependently, their values and beliefs, and the availability of such resources as money, material, and time.

Adult educators must begin to determine which factors affect individual growth, so that we can maximize individual growth and minimize the obstacles to this growth. Thelen (1968, p. vi) argues that "The face-to-face group working on a problem is the meeting ground of individual personality and society. It is in the group that personality is modified and socialized. It is through the working of groups that society is changed and adapted to its times. These two processes are not separate; they are merely two aspects of the same phenomenon. Moreover, they are necessary to each other: without social purposes shared with others there would be no basis for the give-and-take through which the individual develops his capabilities, and without the differences among individual personalities there would be no basis for the creation of new and better solutions to the problems of living."

Thus, as we look at community problem solving, we cannot isolate the individual from the community problem-solving group or the community. We therefore must consider another set of questions: What is the nature of a community problem-solving group's growth? What are the characteristics of community growth? Can we apply the categories we identified for individual growth to describe the growth of the problem-solving group and community? What are the relationships among the educative growth of the individual, the problem-solving group, and the community? The literature on adult education provides few answers to these questions; few researchers have investigated growth from this perspective.

Growth and the Adult Educator

Adult educators are challenged to design transactions that will maximize the educative growth of individuals, problem-solving groups, and communities. Dewey (1938, p. 40) states that "a primary responsibility of educators is that they not only be aware of the general principles of shaping of actual experience by environing conditions but that they also recognize in concrete what surroundings are conducive to having experiences that lead to growth. Above all they should know how to utilize the surroundings, physical and social, that exist so as to extract from them all they have to contribute to building up experiences that are worthwhile."

Research on educative growth in the context of community problem solving has been scant. Campbell (1977) begins to address the ways in which an adult educator can enhance group growth in problem-solving activities. Jimmerson (1977) has sought to clarify the relationship of the adult educator's degree of self-actualization to certain aspects of individual and group growth in problem-solving groups. A survey of the research, however, does not help us to discern the roles and functions the adult educator and others should assume to enhance individual growth in community problem-solving activities. Rather, such a survey generates more questions and untested hypotheses.

Let us return to the proposed chronology of individual growth discussed earlier. If we are correct in hypothesizing that growth in one's stance toward life is prerequisite to further growth, then one essential function of the adult educator and the group's members is to enhance growth in this area. Our primary challenge, therefore, is to help individuals become more open and actively involved in life, to foster individuals' orientation toward the future and their willingness to risk failure. Techniques such as value clarification and consciousness raising, as advocated by Freire (1971) and other theorists, could be useful in this regard.

Once the group members attain a certain degree of intellectual hospitality, the adult educator can work to further enhance the other three categories of individual growth. Studies of community problem-solving groups indicate that techniques such as small group work, "hands-on" experience, and self-evaluation provide opportunities for individual growth. Although the primary reason that group members work together is to solve their community problems, the adult educator's duty is to make the problem-solving process an opportunity for individual, group, and community growth. The educator must employ ingenuity in his selection and implementation of techniques. Further research is needed on specific instructional techniques, their effectiveness in influencing growth, and the specific nature of the types of growth that result. In conducting such research, however, we must not overemphasize the importance of the educator. Individual growth can result from community problem-solving groups that do not involve trained adult educators. The power and the potential of group members to effect their own educational transactions is another area for future research.

Thus vast challenges face adult educators working in the community transactional mode. Now that educators are acknowledging the distinctiveness of this mode, we can no longer evaluate its influence using terms and standards from other disciplines and fields. Rather, we must concern ourselves with the educational character of community problem-solving activities. In this chapter, we have begun this task by raising questions about educative growth. If the educational potential of community problem-solving groups is to be realized, researchers must address questions such as these. We must also begin to define the relationships among educative growth and other areas of growth, such as economic, environmental, and political.

As adult educators, we would be remiss if we failed to respond to one additional challenge: to determine which situations or environments are conducive to educative growth. We must carefully examine the cultural and circumstantial factors that affect the community transactional mode. As Lindeman (1961, postscript) posits, "Life is confronted in the form of situations, occasions which necessitate action. Education is a method for giving situations a setting, for analyzing complex wholes into manageable, understandable parts and a method which points out the path of action which, if followed, will bring out the circumstances within the area of experiment. Since the education is best which most adequately helps us meet situations, the best teaching method is one which emerges from situation-experiences." Community problem solving provides one such situation in which educators may enhance the growth of individuals, groups, and communities.

Comments by the Senior Authors

[1] As we ask who can grow from community problem-solving activities, we see a variety of actors. Coggins states that the community trans-

actional mode may effect growth in individuals, groups, and the larger community. She, like Campbell (Chapter Ten) and Boyd (Chapter Four), asserts that group growth and community growth are different from the sum of the growth experienced by individuals who belong to the group and the community.

We also have individuals in the community who are not actively involved in the community problem-solving processes, but whose lives will probably be touched in some way by these efforts. The community problem-solving group itself represents another actor. As Boyd argues, in Chapter Four, the group is an entity that will develop its own attitudes, processes, relationships, and identity. Similarly, a community—be it a geographical entity or a community defined by common interests—is more than the sum of its constituents. Thus the community as an actor in the community problem-solving process is not synonymous with the sum of the individuals in the community. Lastly, of course, the adult educator is an actor in this activity.

² Just as Coggins has examined relationships among aspects of individual growth, we might also examine relationships among growth in individuals, groups, and their community. To what extent does growth in one of these areas influence growth in the other two? Within the community transactional mode are we apt to see growth occurring in all three areas most of the time? Should adult educators who work in a community setting concentrate their early efforts on individual growth, on group growth, or on community growth?

Part Four

◆◆◆◆◆◆◆◆◆◆◆◆◆◆◆◆◆◆◆◆◆◆◆◆◆
◆◆◆◆◆◆◆◆◆◆◆◆◆◆◆◆◆◆◆◆◆◆◆◆

A Critique
and a Response

◆◆◆◆◆◆◆◆◆◆◆◆◆◆◆◆◆◆◆◆◆◆◆◆◆
◆◆◆◆◆◆◆◆◆◆◆◆◆◆◆◆◆◆◆◆◆◆◆◆

Each of the first three parts of this book has examined one of the three transactional modes. This fourth and final part contains Carlson's critique of the paradigm (Chapter Twelve) and our response to it (Chapter Thirteen). Carlson's chapter provides a critical examination of the paradigm and the ideas presented by the contributors to this volume. In our response, we address some misunderstandings that exist between the authors and Carlson. Our purpose is not to quiet the confrontations but to clarify and focus them.

Carlson presents several criticisms of the model and the contributing authors' applications of it. Carlson views three problems as basic and serious. First, he describes our model as utopian in that we assume that people can and will change their conditions in ways that will enhance everyone's condition if people are given scientific and rational problem-solving techniques. Carlson also criticizes our trust in educational institutions and agencies, claiming that we have given them too large a role in adult education at the expense of noninstitutional and unorganized learning. Carlson believes that most of the contributors to the volume accept this position, and he is afraid most adult educators will accept it as dogma. Carlson sees this as a danger both to adult education and to society. He also criticizes our emphasis on the learner's development of rational problem-solving techniques. Carlson views this approach to educational growth as too narrow.

Carlson affirms the value of pursuing the kinds of basic questions the model raises. In this, we feel we have achieved our principal objective: to provide an open forum for the exchange of different, thoughtful, and provocative positions on the foundational conceptualization of adult education. Chapter Thirteen affords us the opportunity to clarify and argue our positions on the conceptual foundations of adult education.

Chapter Twelve

The Foundation of Adult Education: Analyzing the Boyd-Apps Model

Robert A. Carlson

After studying the preceding eleven chapters, the reader may believe he has some understanding of the foundation of adult education. Certainly that was the objective of this volume. The conceptual model proposed in Chapter One has, however, evoked the expression of only one philosophical approach—a utopian philosophy of adult education that posits the scientific use of institutions to create more perfect individuals and a more perfect society. The authors of this book have examined but a single pillar among the several upon which rests the foundation of adult education as a profession and practice. Alternative philosophies have been relegated to the back of the temple or at least to the back of this book.

In this chapter, we will look at the conceptual model described in Chapter One and developed in the succeeding chapters. We will argue that this model, which the authors consider broadly representative of the foundations of adult education, reflects only one aspect of philosophical thought about education and is, therefore, a dangerously narrow base upon which to structure all of adult education.

Boyd and Apps have developed their conceptual model on utopian values, and these values form a conceptual prison for anyone using their model. They posit as the purpose of all adult education individual, group, and community growth; they define educational growth as the learner's ability to progress through a scientific, rational, problem-solving process. They assume that human beings have the right and the power to change their conditions and will do so in ways that enhance the conditions of all. Such an assumption disregards human helplessness, dependency, irresponsibility, confusion, and irrationality. Their emphasis on the role of institutions in bringing about this growth or change neglects the unavoidable tension between societal and individual interests. Indeed, Boyd and Apps suggest that institutions of adult education can serve the interests of all the people. They appear to assume, or at least to seek, a society in which everyone works to achieve the utopian goal of the happy, harmonious, abundant, rational life. None of the authors strayed far from this lead. Given the reality of contemporary institutional adult education, agents of change could hardly have been given a monopoly of the field. Boyle (Chapter Seven) defines defenders of the status quo as agents of change by describing as agents of change those who intend either to promote change or to prevent change.

The assumptions of this philosophy of adult education cry out for challenge. Is the purpose of education individual and social change, growth, and progress through a scientific, rational, problem-solving process? Do human beings have the right and power to change their conditions? Will the attempted exercise of this assumed power necessarily enhance the conditions of all? Is the definition of education as planned change a worthy concept?

The wanton evil perpetrated by modern, "civilized" man in the twentieth century—often in the name of progress—has led philosophers and social critics to seriously question utopian values.

Although institutions may be able to use scientific, rational, problem-solving processes to implement planned change in the interests of all, contemporary philosophers have asked, as Walsh (1972, p. 16) points out, "whether men are capable of the rationality and goodness to create and sustain" such undertakings. "The verdict is not yet officially rendered," Walsh declares as he reflects on diverse philosophies, "but rumours from the jury-room are not encouraging."

The philosophical premises of the Boyd-Apps model posit the field of adult education as a science that might at last achieve for mankind those elusive utopian goals of happiness, harmony, abundance, and rationality. The model may acknowledge the orneriness of man that has so often disrupted the best-laid utopian plans, but it does not seem to accept that orneriness. Rather, this model appears a neoutopian effort to develop a scientific professional technology to tame that orneriness, to reconstruct man and his society.

Boyd and Apps offer the field one of its first dynamic scientific models. Constructors of a scientific model seek to do more than conceptualize and generate understanding and discussion. They seek ultimately to derive a model that will predict outcomes so that educators can better control adult education activities. Indeed, Boyd has indicated to this author that he views the model as potentially useful for practitioners, as well as for researchers.

The model reflects a vision of adult education as a scientific helping profession. The model's matrix of cells is supposed to assist practitioners in diagnosing different types of educational situations and in prescribing the proper educational treatment for each; researchers are invited to use the model to organize studies that will determine the characteristics of each cell. Such a conception is potentially dangerous. As Walsh propounds in his Law of Reverse Effect, "if you try too hard for something, or try for it at the disregard of other and equally valid goals, you are likely to get the opposite of what you want" (1972, p. 151). The vision of the professional adult educator as diagnostician and prescriber of educational treatment may activate this Law of Reverse Effect, causing a diminution of the very democracy the neoutopian wishes to enhance.

Furthermore, we must ask whether adult education must be conceived of only as a helping profession. An equally valid proposition views adult education as the ball bearings of democracy—the means whereby democracy exists in a welter of competing interests and ideologies. The values underlying this view reject the vision, implicit in the Boyd-Apps model, of society as a cooperative community well-served by institutions of adult education.

In her discussion of community, Wright (Chapter Eight) describes a community's responsibility for the well-being of all its citizens. Some social and educational philosophers are less confident of the responsibilities of humankind, less certain of the altruism of its institutions, and more prone to see society as a discordant, dog-eat-dog struggle among individuals and institutions with competing economic, political, and ideological interests.

Does any community have even a chance of operating in the utopian manner suggested in this book? Must the individual rely primarily on institutions of adult education, as virtually all the contributors except Tough (Chapter Three) seemed to assume, to bring about the growth the individual allegedly ought to desire? Do any institutions of adult education ever serve the interests of all the people?

The contributors clearly place confidence in the institutions of adult education, particularly the authoritative public agency, as serving the best interests of all the people. Boyd and Apps' individual mode in adult education, one might think, would be less dependent upon institutions than the other two modes. But even here Moore (Chapter Two) pictures institutions that deliver instructional programs through various media, and Campbell (Chapter Ten) orients his discussion of group growth to programs sponsored by formal organizations.

The only real challenge to the institutional bias of this model is launched by Tough (Chapter Three). He argues that most adult learning occurs outside the institutional framework and asks why adult educators ignore adult's independent learning efforts and concentrate on groups operated by institutions. Tough's commitment to his view of the individual mode extends the Boyd-Apps model of adult education to include deliberate, self-planned adult learning.

The vast majority of adult education lies beyond the scope of the Boyd-Apps model. Certainly some adult education is carried out by agencies and by educational arms of existing institutions. But even more of it is carried out, often spontaneously, by individuals responding to questions or to their private muse. Most of adult education is unorganized, conducted by peers, poets, propagandists, priests, peddlers, politicians, performers, publishers, pamphleteers, playwrights, publicans, and practitioners of the plastic arts.

Virtually all conceptual models developed by theoreticians of adult education ignore or downplay this unorganized aspect of the field. Only Ohliger (1974a) in his interpretation of Illich's dichotomy between official knowledge and personal knowledge, has come close to developing a countermodel. Ohliger pleads the case for spontaneous, random, chance, unplanned learning that is the great joy and sorrow of our human existence. Unorganized, unplanned learning and spontaneous independent adult education, neither directed by agencies, constitute perhaps three fourths of all adult educational activities.

Only the remaining fourth of adult education is described by the Boyd-Apps model. Their model may be useful for an analysis of formal and informal institutional adult education and deliberate self-planned adult learning. Institutions offer formal adult programs at three levels: basic education, which includes skills for living and reading, writing, and arithmetic; secondary adult education, which includes high school equivalency programs, vocational education for adults, and such programs as English as a second language; and postsecondary adult education, which includes university extension programs and continuing professional education.

Most activity in this organized sector of adult education, however, is deliberate, self-planned adult learning. Quite effective in this sector are informal institutional programs, programs conducted by such institutions as voluntary agencies, government organizations, political parties and organizations, religious groups, and other such organizations. The most crucial of these institutions to the preservation of democracy may well be the voluntary self-interest groups that urge their economic, political, or ideological interests upon the public for general acceptance. In many communities, groups with opposing views publicly confront and debate one another in an effort to sway public opinion. Their sublimated warfare, which is conducted through informal agencies and—even more crucial to democratic freedom—through the three fourths of adult education independent of institutions, is the pillar of adult education that is, perhaps, the most meaningful aspect of the field. Yet the view of adult education implicit in the Boyd-Apps model excludes all such activities.

Professional adult educators have usually defined unorganized adult education as incidental, accidental, or chance education or learning and have denigrated it as inferior to organized and deliberate adult education. Indeed, Campbell (Chapter Ten) contends that unanticipated learning is not adult education, that education is learning that results from planning. When one considers one's own education, however, one may well recognize that the most meaningful learning has resulted from this unorganized component. Seller (1978) describes one example of unorganized, unplanned adult education: the educational opportunities for immigrants to the United States between 1914 and 1924. She says, "The Finnish boarding house, the Greek or Armenian coffee house, the local candy store, the ubiquitous corner saloon—these and similar natural gathering places served as informal classrooms where 'oldtimers' taught newcomers a few basic English words, how to get a job, where to find help in case of illness or other crises, what local politicians could be relied upon for various services, and which American laws were enforced and which could be broken with inpunity. The night school taught American ideals; the saloon keeper taught American realities" (p. 89).

This example compels us to reexamine the trust that Boyd and Apps place in organizations and institutions. Whom should the individual trust: a professional adult educator, who tends to represent one or another of the vested institutional interests, or a representative of unorganized adult education, in this case, the saloon keeper? The immigrants often chose the saloon keeper and were probably wise in doing so.

Unorganized adult education plays a crucial role in preserving choice, in offering alternatives, in contending with attempts at social control by institutional adult education. There

are still ubiquitous saloon keepers; like professional adult educators, some of them are effective and others are not. In addition to
saloon keepers, we have playwrights, songwriters, public gadflies,
and others who seek to teach us. Although Boyd and Apps contend
that all endeavors in adult education may be located on their
model, the activity of the saloon keeper, the artist, and the soapbox
orator do not belong in any of the cells. Yet surely such unorganized educational experiences are not inferior to those adult
students receive in a community college course in shorthand and
typing or a correspondence course in letter writing. One cannot,
however, identify a concert of political music by any of the cells of
the Boyd-Apps model. Are we thus to assume that performing
artists cannot be adult educators? Or is the model too narrow?

Some parts of unorganized adult education may be made to
fit within the model. Certainly Davie (Chapter Nine), who recognizes the social struggle among different interest groups, initially
leaves an opening for minority group leaders and some political
party organizers as agents of education. But, locked into the
conceptual prison of the model, Davie immediately ascribes to
these community organizers' institutional roles with social action
agencies. This development should cause reflection upon the rami-
fications of urging acceptance of unorganized adult education
within the cells of this model.

Davie's well-meaning openness exemplifies the conundrum
facing those who embrace values supported by other philosophical
pillars of adult education and yet try to work within this model.
The utopian philosophy permeating the model is aggressive, im-
perialistic, coopting. As Tough (Chapter Three) suggests, there
is some danger that professional adult educators will attempt to
dominate all forms of adult learning, thereby forcing everyone to
conform to their ideals and standards. Although Tough trusts that
some undefined forces will prevent the entire field from domina-
tion by the values of a single philosophy of adult education, others
are less confident of these safeguards. Tough calls for the adult
educator to respect the integrity of the adult learner, to provide
services that people may choose or reject without penalty. But
those committed to the utopian vision of adult education are dedicated to bringing about change (or to preserving the status quo)

and to propagating their faith in growth through problem solving. Can we trust them to honor the learner's autonomy and to forgo efforts to institutionalize and rationalize the unorganized, unplanned areas of adult education? Would the inclusion of unorganized adult education in the Boyd-Apps model result in professional educators' attempts to evaluate and harmonize the work of unorganized practitioners in terms of currently popular public policy?

A utopian philosophy of education that emphasizes professional practice and either overlooks or attempts to regulate independent, unorganized, and nonprofessional activities is dangerous. A model that excludes three fourths of adults' educational activities is not an adequate representation of the field. The Boyd-Apps model is neither all-encompassing nor objective. It is based on utopian values that have become enshrined as dogma in adult education. Although utopianists cite research to support their dogma, that research was designed according to the principles of the dogma.

Boyd and Apps make a number of claims for the value and usefulness of their model. They assert that it unites instruction and curriculum, that it enables the analyst to explore the influences of social and cultural systems on educational activities. Their conception of adult education as a transactional activity is the most valuable contribution of their model. But readers must compare this contribution with the negative potential of the model.

The other three claims Boyd and Apps make for their model must also be challenged. They claim that their model provides a tool for the identification of problems in adult education. This very concern for diagnosing "problems" reflects a philosophical bias that views scientific intervention as appropriate to all areas of human interaction, even when such interference may destroy the humane essence of those interactions. This mechanistic model reflects the ideal that adult educators should strive to be the social equivalent of medical doctors. Sork (1977) envisions a day when adult educators will diagnose and treat community educational needs. He calls on educators to develop normative values and social indicators against which "disease" could be tested. If a community's social indicators strayed from the norm, the adult educators would treat the "symptoms" and help the community return to "normal." Sork urges educators to adopt not only a curative role but also a preventive one as they tend to the community's "educational health." Yet, Sork could not offer any assurance that the adult educators' cure would not be worse than the symptoms.

Similarly, Coggins (Chapter Eleven) urges the adult educator to help individuals become more open, more actively involved in life, more oriented to the future, and more willing to risk failure. She does not question the ethics of such goals and does not seem to recognize that the normality, objectivity, or desirability of these goals are debatable. These values are advanced, unexamined, as worthy indicators of normality because they fit the utopian vision of the happy, harmonious, abundant, rational life that the Boyd-Apps model assumes.

The other two claims for this model, that it shifts emphasis away from the disciplines and contributes to defining an identity for adult education, are either incorrect or unsound. Boyd and Apps hold that their model achieves an accurate assessment of the foundation of adult education by, at least in part, standing independent of the social sciences and philosophy. To the contrary, the model's vision of the entire field of adult education is based upon utopian philosophical thought. The authors have not shifted emphasis from the disciplines at all; they have merely narrowed the selection of materials to be borrowed. The identity they achieve is unsound—narrow, unidimensional, and one-pillared.

The definition of the field offered by Boyd and Apps threatens to weaken the very democracy it intends to enhance. By identifying adult education in this one philosophical framework, they have packaged the adult educator as a physician-salesman, affiliated with an institution, who offers coping skills for solving problems within the constraints of the existing power structure. To the extent that a client solves his problems within this framework, progress or growth are said to have occurred. The model is thus basically a technicist one that establishes norms for behavior and growth. It could serve as a blueprint for adult educators who wish to be the technicians of a Brave New World or 1984.

Our final judgment of the model will depend, of course, on how it is used. If the model initiates discussion that results in a rich mosaic of identity for the field of adult education, then the exercise of building this model will be of value. However, scientific models are usually used in the design of research that is then compared with research based on competing scientific models in order for theorists to determine which provides the most effective results. The modern imperative to discover the one most efficient technique inevitably presses toward the adoption of one model by all practitioners; indeed, to be a member of a professional field is to adopt certain codes that define that field. We must, therefore, recognize the philosophical limitations, the neoutopian blinders, this model would impose on research and practice in adult education if we allow it to define the field.

Theorists and practitioners who understand other philosophies of adult education must develop a range of philosophical models of adult education that challenge the assumptions of the neoutopians. We need definitions of the field that do not rely solely on such terms as *change, growth, progress,* and *problem solving*. We need a theory that honors the orneriness that is humankind, that provides an esteemed place for unorganized and unplanned adult education, that accepts the conflicts of interests inherent in all societies, that recognizes the finite nature of planning, and that takes account of the limits both to man's rationality and to his scientific technology. Such a theory might challenge the conception of the field as an independent helping profession. It may be that one of the most effective ways to preserve and strengthen the democratic system is to conceptualize adult education as a field of study and practice engaged in by members of many professions and individuals involved in community service or in the promotion of competing ideological, political, and economic interests. This view honors adult education as a marginal activity of many individuals and institutions, rather than as a profession in and of itself.

The Boyd-Apps model is a potentially prescriptive, technicist tool for research and practice. The philosophical pillar that supports the model is but one pillar of the foundation of adult education. We need a more accurate, many pillared representation of the foundation of adult education and serious discussion of the continuing challenges various philosophies offer one another. Educators should not view the debate over the choice of a model as merely an intramural skirmish in adult education. Our definitions of our field, our methodology, and our goals affect not only our activities but those of all individuals, groups, and communities who participate in any form of learning. Because adult education is an activity essential to the functioning of a democratic society, we cannot be content with a partial understanding of it.

Chapter Thirteen

◆◆◆◆◆◆◆◆◆◆◆◆◆◆◆◆◆◆◆◆◆◆◆◆◆◆◆◆◆
◆◆◆◆◆◆◆◆◆◆◆◆◆◆◆◆◆◆◆◆◆◆◆◆◆◆

Response

◆◆◆◆◆◆◆◆◆◆◆◆◆◆◆◆◆◆◆◆◆◆◆◆◆◆
◆◆◆◆◆◆◆◆◆◆◆◆◆◆◆◆◆◆◆◆◆◆◆◆◆◆

Jerold W. Apps
Robert D. Boyd

Our intent in proposing our model is not to place a final word before our readers but to provoke discussion among adult educators. We consider our conceptual framework and the chapters written by our associates as inaugurating an important discussion of the foundations of adult education. We began our work knowing that some educators would disagree and hoping that such disagreement would lead to productive discussion of the many difficulties adult educators face.

Within this spirit of disagreement and discussion, in this chapter, we respond to several of the criticisms made by Carlson in Chapter Twelve. We have selected those criticisms that we believe are based on misinterpretations or misunderstandings of our analysis and those criticisms that represent the differences between our assumptions and Carlson's about the purposes of this book. We focus our attention on Carlson's criticisms of the book as a whole and his objections to the model proposed in Chapter One; we do not discuss his criticisms of the contributing authors' analyses.

We believe that Carlson has misinterpreted the parts of Chapter One that describe the differences between education and learning, and between institutional and noninstitutional adult education. Let us now be more explicit and clarify the differences between the terms *education* and *learning*. We argue that there are two kinds of learning, that which is planned and that which just happens. The latter may be called *incidental,* or *accidental,* or *chance,* or *random learning.*

A successful educational endeavor results in planned learning, and it usually also results in a good deal of random learning. But random learning may be effected by many experiences; it may result from listening to music, talking to the neighborhood bartender, or simply walking around the block. Random learning is indeed important, but planned learning is the special province and goal of educational endeavors. In this book, our attention is focused on education and, more specifically, adult education. Thus we concentrate on that education which is primarily concerned with planned learning. We do not discount the contributions made to random learning by artists, novelists, or public figures. But, according to our definition, these persons are not educators because their primary intention was not to generate planned learning. Our argument is not that because these people lack credentials as adult educators their activities cannot be educational ones. Rather, we argue that these people have not, in most instances, consciously intended that learning should occur. Only people who consciously plan for learning are conducting adult education, according to our definition.

Thus, Carlson's term *unorganized education* is, for us a paradox. Education is a plan for learning, and activities that are planned are not unorganized. Institutions and agencies, however, do not have a monopoly on organizing learning activities. Any agency, institution, individual, group, or community can organize adult education activities. Churches, museums, service clubs, groups of neighbors, poetry lovers, and noontime joggers have the potential to provide adult education. It does not matter if a group is commonly thought of as an institution of adult education; nor does it matter if any of the participants are designated adult educators by training or experience. The criterion for an adult education activity is whether the individual or group has developed a plan for learning.

We could have included more examples of adult education that are independent of institutions and agencies. The sparse number of examples apparently has led Carlson to conclude that our model is promoting only professional adult education. We believe, however, that our conceptual framework is useful not only for our understanding of the totality of adult education but also for the design of programs to train adult educators. Researchers can use the model to identify questions and design studies that will increase the body of knowledge for the profession of adult education.

We see a difference, though, between the profession of adult education and the field of adult education. The profession of adult education includes those persons who are trained as teachers, researchers, or scholars in adult education. The field of adult education includes the professionals and nonprofessionals who practice adult education; it includes educational institutions and all other institutions that from time to time sponsor adult education activities; and it includes learning that is not institutionally sponsored, learning planned and organized by individuals and by ad hoc groups. Our framework for adult education comprises all sectors of adult education, not just that rather small portion sponsored by institutions and carried out by professional adult educators.

Having adequately discussed Carlson's misunderstanding of our view of institutionalized adult education, we must say a few words about his criticism of our utopianism. Carlson delineates four implicit assumptions of our work: (1) Education constitutes planned individual and social growth and progress through a scientific, rational, problem-solving process; (2) People have the right and power to change their conditions and will do so in ways that enhance the conditions of all; (3) One can trust institutions to effect change in the interests of all people; (4) Adult education is a helping profession whose practitioners seek to diagnose educational problems and prescribe proper educational treatment for them.

Carlson's summary approximates our basic assumptions, although we would quibble a bit with some of his interpretation. We do not, however, consider our premises to be utopian; rather, we feel they are reasonable assumptions upon which adult educators can posit their understanding of the field. Let us briefly review each point of Carlson's critique.

Carlson asserts that we have granted rationality too predominant a role. We believe that learners gain knowledge in ways other than by use of rational, problem-solving processes. We do not discount the educational value of artistic endeavor, and we find educational value in the raising of the learner's consciousness. The learner's purpose in broadening his awareness, however, is not solely to become aware of new ideas but to make some use of the insights gained. In order to use his insights, for whatever purpose, the learner will have recourse to rational processes.

As Carlson states, we do believe that people have the right and the power to change their conditions. If people share this power in open, educational transactions, the resulting changes will benefit all. We do not consider this view utopian; we maintain, in contrast, that this position must be a premise valued by all educators in a democratic society.

Our trust in institutions is neither unquestioning nor absolute. We believe that we can trust institutions only if the relationships between institutions and individuals are transactional, and only if we are willing to change our institutions when necessary. Institutions are forms that people create and that people can change; institutions can be humane and responsive.

Lastly, Carlson is correct in stating that we believe that education is a helping profession. We reject, however the medical model of diagnosis and treatment as inappropriate to our profession. Throughout this volume, education is depicted as a transactional activity. Unlike the usual relationship between doctor and patient, the transactional relationship between educator and learner is a cooperative effort. (Enlightened medical practice can follow a transactional ideal in the sense that the physician helps the patient heal himself.)

Carlson raises a number of provocative questions about the characteristics of adults and the nature of adult learning. Our focus precludes a consideration of such topics as the psychology of the mature adult. Carlson's excellent questions will have to await further research.

In conclusion, we restate our initial intentions for this volume, trusting our readers to evaluate our contribution to the field. We sought to define the field and practice of adult education by (1) providing a mechanism for the identification and organization of problems in adult education; (2) discouraging adult educators from the indiscriminate borrowing of concepts from other disciplines; (3) offering a model that unites the concepts of curriculum and instruction; and (4) proposing an analytic method that stresses the relevance of social, cultural, and personal systems for educational plans and activities.

References

ABSHIER, G. S. "The Demonstration Approach." In H. B. Long, R. C. Anderson, and J. A. Blubaugh (Eds.), *Approaches to Community Development*. Iowa City, Iowa: American College Testing Program, 1973.

AIKEN, H. D. *Reason and Conduct: New Bearings in Moral Philosophy*. New York: Knopf, 1962.

ALINSKY, S. D. *Rules for Radicals: A Practical Primer for Realistic Radicals*. New York: Vintage Books, 1971.

ALLPORT, G. W. *Becoming*. New Haven, Conn.: Yale University Press, 1955.

ALMOND, G. A. *American People and Foreign Policy*. New York: Praeger, 1960.

ANDERSON, S. B., BALL, S., MURPHY, R. T., and ASSOCIATES. *Encyclopedia of Educational Evaluation: Concepts and Techniques for Evalu-*

ating Education and Training Programs. San Francisco: Jossey-Bass, 1975.

ASCH, S. E. *Social Psychology.* Englewood Cliffs, N.J.: Prentice-Hall, 1952.

ASCH, S. E. "Studies of Independence and Conformity: A Minority of One Against a Unanimous Majority." *Psychological Monographs,* 1956, *70,* 9.

ASCH, S. E. "A Perspective on Social Psychology." In Koch (Ed.), *Psychology: A Study of a Science,* Volume 3. New York: McGraw-Hill, 1959.

AUSUBEL, D. P. *Educational Psychology: A Cognitive View.* New York: Holt, Rinehart and Winston, 1968.

BALES, R. F. *Interaction Process Analysis: A Method for the Study of Small Groups.* Reading, Mass.: Addison-Wesley, 1950.

BALES, R. F. *Personality and Interpersonal Behavior.* New York: Holt, Rinehart and Winston, 1970.

BALES, R. F., and STRODTBECK, F. L. "Phases in Group Problem Solving." *Journal of Abnormal Social Psychology,* 1951, *46,* 485–495.

BANNISTER, R. E. *Comparison of Two History Instruction Methods: Radio Broadcasting and Visual Aids Versus Individualized Instruction with Audio-Visual Aids, Final Report.* ERIC ED 032 783. Bethesda, Md.: ERIC Document Reproduction Service, 1969.

BASKIN, S., and KEETON, M. "A Comment on 'The Use of Independent Study Programs.' " *Journal of Higher Education,* February 1962, *33,* 104–106.

BECKER, H. S. (Ed.). *Social Problems: A Modern Approach.* New York: Wiley, 1966.

BEGGS, D. W., and BUFFIE, E. G. (Eds.). *Independent Study.* Bloomington: Indiana University Press, 1965.

BENNE, K. D., and SHEATS, P. "Functional Roles of Group Members." *Journal of Social Issues,* 1948, *4,* 41–49.

BENNETT, C. F., and NELSON, D. L. *Analyzing Impacts of Community Development.* U.S.D.A. Extension Service, Mississippi State, Miss.: Southern Rural Development Center, 1975.

BENNIS, W. G. "Patterns and Vicissitudes in T-Group Development." In L. P. Bradford and others (Eds.), *T-Group Theory and Laboratory Method.* New York: Wiley, 1964.

BENNIS, W. G., and SHEPARD, H. A. "A Theory of Group Development." *Human Relations,* 1956, *9,* 415–417.

BENNIS, W. G., and OTHERS. (Eds.). *The Planning of Change.* (3rd ed.) New York: Holt, Rinehart and Winston, 1961.

"Berger Report Impressive." *Star-Phoenix* (Saskatoon, Saskatchewan, Canada), May 12, 1977, p. 23.

BIDDLE, B. J., and THOMAS, E. J. (Eds.). *Role Theory: Concepts and Research.* New York: Wiley, 1966.

BIDDLE, W. W., and BIDDLE, L. J. *The Community Development Process: The Rediscovery of Local Initiative.* New York: Holt, Rinehart and Winston, 1965.

BIGGE, M. L. *Learning Theories for Teachers.* (3rd ed.) New York: Harper & Row, 1976.

BION, W. R. *Experiences in Groups.* New York: Basic Books, 1959.

BLAKELY, R. J. "What Is Adult Education?" In M. S. Knowles (Ed.), *Handbook of Adult Education in the United States.* Chicago: Adult Education Association, 1960.

BLITZ, A., and SMITH, T. "Personality Characteristics and Performance of Computer Assisted Instruction and Programmed Text." Paper presented at American Educational Research Association Annual Meeting, New Orleans, February 1973.

BODE, B. H. *Modern Educational Theories.* New York: Vintage Books, 1927.

BOONE, E. J. "The Cooperative Extension Service." In R. M. Smith, G. F. Aker, and J. R. Kidd (Eds.), *Handbook of Adult Education.* New York: Macmillan, 1970.

BOYD, R. D. "Psychological Definition of Adult Education." *Adult Leadership,* 1966, *15,* 160–162.

BOYD, R. D. "General Principles of Teaching at the University Level." In L. E. Bone (Ed.), *Library Education: An International Survey.* Urbana: University of Illinois, 1968.

BOYD, R. D. "The Molecular Model." Unpublished manuscript. Madison: University of Wisconsin, 1969.

BOYD, R. D., and WILSON, J. P. "Three Channel Theory of Communication in Small Groups." *Adult Education,* 1974, *24,* (3), 167–183.

BOYLE, P. G. *The Program Planning Processes With Emphasis on Extension.* NAECAS Publication No. 24. Madison: University of Wisconsin, 1965.

BROWN, B. *Delphi Process: A Methodology Used for the Elicitation of Opinions of Experts.* Santa Monica, Calif.: RAND Corporation, 1968.

BRUNER, J. S. *Toward a Theory of Instruction.* New York: Norton, 1966.

BRUNER, J. S., and TAJFEL, H. "Cognitive Risk and Environmental Change." *Journal of Abnormal and Social Psychology,* 1961, *62,* 231–241.

BRYSON, L. *Adult Education.* New York: American Book Company, 1936.

BRYSON, L. "What We Mean by Adult Education." In M. Ely (Ed.), *Handbook of Adult Education in the United States.* New York: Institute of Adult Education, Teachers College, Columbia University, 1948.

BUCHANAN, N. S., and ELLIS, H. *Approaches to Economic Development.* New York: Twentieth Century Fund, 1955.

CAMPBELL, M. D., JR. "Musings: Part One." Unpublished paper. Madison: Department of Continuing and Vocational Education, University of Wisconsin, 1976.

CAMPBELL, M. D., JR. "The Influence of the Adult Educator on Group Growth in Community Problem Solving." Unpublished doctoral dissertation, University of Wisconsin, 1977.

CANTRILL, H. *The Pattern of Human Concerns.* New Brunswick, N.J.: Rutgers University Press, 1965.

CARLSON, E. R. "Attitude Change Through Modification of Attitude Structure." *Journal of Abnormal and Social Psychology,* 1956, *52,* 265–267.

CARLSON, R. A. "A Graying of the Campus." *Review of Education,* September–October 1977a, *3,* 5.

CARLSON, R. A. "Professionalization of Adult Education: An Historical-Philosophical Analysis," *Adult Education,* 1977b, *28* (1).

CARLSON, R. A. Speech at the Pennsylvania State University, April 1977c.

CARTWRIGHT, D., and ZANDER, A. (Eds.). *Group Dynamics: Research & Theory.* New York: Harper & Row, 1968.

CARY, L. J. *Community Development as a Process.* Columbia: University of Missouri Press, 1970.

CATTELL, R. B. "Concepts and Methods in Measurement of Group Syntality." *Psychological Review,* 1948, *55,* 48–63.

CHAPIN, F. S., JR. *Urban Land Use Planning.* Urbana: University of Illinois Press, 1963.

CHICKERING, A. W. "Dimensions of Independence." *Journal of Higher Education,* January 1964, *25,* 38–41.

CHIN, R. "Some Ideas on Changing." In R. I. Miller (Ed.), *Perspective for Educational Change.* New York: Appleton-Century-Crofts, 1965.

CLARK, T. (Ed.). *Community Structure and Decision Making: Comparative Analysis.* San Francisco: Chandler, 1968.

CLARKE, K. M. "Independent Study, a Concept Analysis." *Proceedings of a Conference on Independent Learning.* W. K. Kellogg Foundation Report, No. 7. Vancouver: University of British Columbia Adult Education Research Centre, 1973.

COCH, L., and FRENCH, J., JR. "Overcoming Resistance to Change." In G. E. Swanson and others (Eds.), *Readings in Social Psychology.* New York: Holt, 1952.

COGGINS, C. C. "Toward a Definition of Individual Growth in the Rural Community Problem Solving Context." Unpublished doctoral dissertation, University of Wisconsin, 1976.

COHEN, J. W. "On Independent Study: The Need to Clarify Its Role in Higher Education." *Journal of Higher Education,* February 1962, *32,* 103–104.

CONGER, D. S. *Canadian Open Adult Learning Systems.* Prince Albert, Saskatchewan, Canada: Department of Manpower and Immigration, 1974.

COOLICAN, P. M. *Self-Planned Learning: Implications for the Future of Adult Education.* ERIC ED 095 254. Syracuse, N.Y.: Educational Policy Research Center, Syracuse University Research Corporation, 1974.

DAVIDOFF, P., and REINER, T. "A Choice Theory of Planning." *Journal of the American Institute of Planning,* 1962, *28,* 105–112.

DAVIE, L. E. "Ericksonian Ego Crises Theory Applies to Small Group Progression." Unpublished doctoral dissertation, University of Wisconsin, 1971.

DAVIE, L. E., and OTHERS. *SHAPES: Handbook.* Toronto: Ontario

Institute for Studies in Education, Department of Adult Education, 1975.

DENYS, L. O. J. *The Major Learning Efforts of Two Groups of Accra Adults.* Unpublished doctoral dissertation, Ontario Institute for Studies in Education, University of Toronto, 1973.

DEUTSCH, M., and KRAUSS, R. M. *Theories in Social Psychology.* New York: Basic Books, 1965.

DEWEY, J. *Democracy and Education.* New York: Macmillan, 1916.

DEWEY, J. *Experience and Education.* New York: Macmillan, 1938.

DEWEY, J. *The School and Society.* Chicago: University of Chicago Press, 1956.

DEWEY, J., "Means-Ends." In R. D. Archambault (Ed.), *John Dewey on Education: Selected Writings.* New York: Modern Library, 1964.

DEWEY, J., and BENTLEY, A. F. *Knowing and the Known.* Boston: Beacon Press, 1949.

DRESSEL, P. L., and THOMPSON, M. M. *Independent Study: A New Interpretation of Concepts, Practices, and Problems.* San Francisco: Jossey-Bass, 1973.

DUNN, E. *Economic and Social Development: A Process of Social Learning.* Baltimore: Johns Hopkins Press, 1971.

ERICKSON, C., and CHAUSOW, H. *Chicago's TV Colleges, Final Report of a Three Year Experiment of the Chicago City Junior College in Offering College Courses for Credit Via Open Circuit Television.* ERIC ED 021 442. Bethesda, Md.: ERIC Document Reproduction Service, 1960.

ERIKSON, E. H. *Childhood and Society.* New York: Norton, 1950.

ETZIONI, A. *The Active Society.* New York: Free Press, 1968.

FAIR, J. "Teachers as Learners: The Learning Projects of Beginning Elementary School Teachers." Unpublished doctoral dissertation, University of Toronto, 1973.

FARQUHARSON, A. *Peers as Helpers: Personal Change in Members of Self-Help Groups in Metropolitan Toronto.* Unpublished doctoral dissertation, Ontario Institute for Studies in Education, University of Toronto, 1973.

FAURE, E., and OTHERS. *Learning to Be: The World of Education, Today and Tomorrow.* Paris: UNESCO, 1972.

FENICHEL, O. *The Psychoanalytic Theory of Neurosis.* New York: Norton, 1945.

FESTINGER, L. *A Theory of Cognitive Dissonance.* Evanston, Ill.: Row, Peterson, 1957.

FESTINGER, L., and ARONSON, E. "The Arousal and Reduction of Dissonance in Social Context." In D. Cartwright and A. Zander (Eds.), *Group Dynamics: Research & Theory.* Evanston, Ill.: Row, Peterson, 1968.

FIEDLER, F. E., and MEUWESE, W. A. T. "Leader's Contribution to Task Performance in Cohesive and Uncohesive Groups." *Journal of Abnormal and Social Psychology,* 1963, *67,* 83–87.

FLANDERS, N. A. *Analyzing Teaching Behavior.* Menlo Park, Calif.: Addison-Wesley, 1970.

FOREST, L. B. "Present Commitments: Their Relationship to One's Acceptance of Community Change and Programs." *Adult Education,* 1973, *23* (3), 171–191.

FRANKL, V. E. *Man's Search for Meaning.* Boston: Beacon Press, 1959.

FRANKLIN, R. *Toward the Style of the Community Change Educator.* Washington, D.C.: National Training Laboratory Institute for Applied Behavioral Science, 1969.

FRANKLIN, R., and FRANKLIN, P. *Tomorrow's Track: Experiments with Learning to Change.* Columbia, Md.: New Community Press, 1976.

FREIRE, P. *Pedagogy of the Oppressed.* New York: Herder and Herder, 1970.

FREUD, A. *The Ego and Mechanisms of Defense.* (Rev. ed.) New York: International Universities Press, 1963.

FREUD, S. *Group Psychology and the Analysis of the Ego.* London: Hogarth Press, 1922.

FREUD, S. *Inhibitions, Symptoms, and Anxiety.* (J. Strachey, Ed.) New York: Norton, 1926.

FREUD, S. *An Outline of Psychoanalysis.* (J. Strachey, Ed.) New York: Norton, 1969.

FROMM, E. *The Revolution of Hope.* New York: Harper & Row, 1968.

GAGNÉ, R. M. *The Conditions of Learning.* New York: Holt, Rinehart and Winston, 1965.

GALLAHER, A., JR., and SANTOPOLO, F. A. "Perspectives on Agent Roles." *Journal of Cooperative Extension,* 1967, *5,* 223–230.

GARDNER, J. W. *Self-Renewal.* New York: Harper & Row, 1965.

GARDNER, R. W., and LONG, R. I. "The Stability of Cognitive Controls." *Journal of Abnormal and Social Psychology,* 1962, *53,* 129–140.

GARDNER, R. W., and OTHERS. "Cognitive Control: A Study of Individual Consistencies in Cognitive Behavior." *Psychological Issues,* 1959, (entire issue).

GIBB, C. A. "Leadership." In G. Lindzey (Ed.), *Handbook of Social Psychology.* Cambridge, Mass.: Addison-Wesley, 1965.

GLASER, B. G., and STRAUSS, A. L. *The Discovery of Grounded Theory: Strategies for Qualitative Research.* Chicago: Aldine, 1967.

GLEASON, G. T. (Ed.). *The Theory and Nature of Independent Learning.* Scranton, Pa.: International Textbook, 1967.

GOULD, S. B., and CROSS, K. P. (Eds.). *Explorations in Non-Traditional Study.* San Francisco: Jossey-Bass, 1972.

GOULDNER, A. W. *The Dialectic of Ideology and Technology.* New York: Seabury Press, 1976.

GRATTAN, C. H. *In Quest of Knowledge: A Historical Perspective on Adult Education.* New York: Association Press, 1955.

GROSS, R. *The Lifelong Learner.* New York: Simon & Schuster, 1977.

GRUEN, W. "A Pragmatic Criticism of Community-Centered Adult Education." *Adult Education,* 1956, *6,* 81–90.

HAAN, N. "Proposed Model of Ego Functioning: Coping and Defense Mechanisms in Relationship to IQ Change." *Psychological Monographs,* 1963, *77* (entire issue).

HAAN, N. "A Tripartite Model of Ego Functioning Values and Clinical and Research Applications." *Journal of Nervous and Mental Diseases,* 1969, *1,* 148.

HARDIN, G., "The Tragedy of the Commons." *Science,* 1968, *162,* 1243–1248.

HARDIN, G. *Exploring New Ethics for Survival.* New York: Viking, 1972.

HARTMANN, H. "Ego Psychology and the Problem of Adaptation." In A. Rapaport (Ed.), *The Organization and Pathology of Thought.* New York: Columbia University Press, 1951.

HAVELOCK, R. G. *Planning for Innovation.* Ann Arbor: Institute for Social Research, University of Michigan, 1971.

HAVELOCK, R. G. *The Change Agent's Guide to Innovation in Education.* Englewood Cliffs, N.J.: Educational Technology Publications, 1973.

HAVIGHURST, R. J. *Developmental Tasks and Education.* (3rd ed.) New York: McKay, 1972.

HEATHERS, G. "Acquiring Dependence and Independence: A Theoretical Orientation." *Journal of Genetic Psychology,* 1955, *87,* 277–291.

HELMER, O. *The Use of the Delphi Technique in Problems of Educational Innovations.* Santa Monica, Calif.: RAND Corporation, 1966.

HENDERSON, K. G. "A Theoretical Model for Teaching." *School Review,* Winter 1964, *73,* 384–391.

HESBURGH, T. M., MILLER, P. A., and WHARTON, C. R. *Patterns for Lifelong Learning.* San Francisco: Jossey-Bass, 1973.

HIEMSTRA, R. "The Educative Community in Action." *Adult Leadership,* 1975a, *24* (3), 82–85.

HIEMSTRA, R. *The Older Adult and Learning.* ERIC ED 117 371. Lincoln: Department of Adult and Continuing Education, University of Nebraska, 1975b.

HIEMSTRA, R. *Lifelong Learning.* Lincoln, Nebr.: Professional Educators Publications, 1976.

HILGARD, E. R. *Theories of Learning.* (4th ed.) Englewood Cliffs, N.J.: Prentice-Hall, 1975.

HOFFER, W. "Defensive Process and Defensive Organization: Their Place in Psychoanalytic Techniques." *International Journal of Psychoanalysis,* 1954, *35,* 194–198.

HOLMBERG, B. "Educational Technology and Correspondence Education." In R. Erdos (Ed.), *Proceedings of the Eighth International Conference of the International Council on Correspondence Education.* Paris: International Council on Correspondence Education, 1969.

HOLMBERG, B. *Distance Education.* New York: Nichols, 1977.

HOSELITZ, B. F. "Noneconomic Barriers to Economic Development." *Economic Development and Cultural Change,* 1952, *1,* 8–21.

HOULE, C. O. *The Inquiring Mind.* Madison: University of Wisconsin Press, 1961.

HOULE, C. O. "The Emergence of Graduate Study in Adult Education." In G. Jensen, A. A. Liveright, and W. Hallenback (Eds.), *Adult Education: Outline of an Emerging Field of University Study.* Washington, D.C.: Adult Education Association, 1964.

HOULE, C. O. *The External Degree.* San Francisco: Jossey-Bass, 1973.

HULL, C. L. *Principles of Behavior.* New York: Appleton-Century-Crofts, 1943.

INSKO, C. A. *Theories of Attitude Change.* New York: Appleton-Century-Crofts, 1967.

JACKSON, P. "The Way Teaching Is." In R. Hyman (Ed.), *Contemporary Thought on Teaching.* Englewood Cliffs, N.J.: Prentice-Hall, 1971.

JANIS, I. L. *Victims of Groupthink.* Boston: Houghton Mifflin, 1972.

JENSEN, G. E. "How Adult Education Borrows and Reformulates Knowledge of Other Disciplines." In G. Jensen, A. A. Liveright, and W. Hallenback (Eds.), *Adult Education: Outlines of an Emerging Field of University Study.* Washington, D.C.: Adult Education Association, 1964.

JENSEN, G. E., LIVERIGHT, A. A., and HALLENBACK, W. (Eds.). *Adult Education: Outlines of an Emerging Field of University Study.* Washington, D.C.: Adult Education Association, 1964.

JIMMERSON, R. "The Relationship Between the Adult Educator's Self-Actualization and Growth in Community Problem Solving." Unpublished doctoral dissertation, University of Wisconsin, 1977.

JOHNS, W. E. "Selected Characteristics of the Learning Projects Pursued by Practicing Pharmacists." Unpublished doctoral dissertation, University of Georgia, 1973.

JOHNSON, E. "Selected Characteristics of the Learning Projects Pursued by Adults Who Have Earned a High School Diploma and/or a High School Equivalency Certificate." Unpublished doctoral dissertation, University of Georgia, 1973.

JOHNSON, E. I. *Metroplex Assembly: An Experiment in Community, An Experiment in Community Education.* Chicago: Center for the Study of Liberal Education for Adults, 1941.

JUNG, C. G., "Analytical Psychology and Education." In *Collected Works.* Vol. 17: *The Development of Personality.* London: Routledge & Kegan Paul, 1954.

KAHN, R. L., and KATZ, D. "Leadership Practices in Relation to Productivity and Morale." In D. Cartwright and A. Zander (Eds.), *Group Dynamics: Research & Theory.* New York: Harper & Row, 1968.

KAPLAN, A. "Public Affairs Education." In M. S. Knowles (Ed.),

Handbook of Adult Education. Chicago: Adult Education Association, 1960.

KATZ, D., and STOTLAND, E. "A Preliminary Statement to a Theory of Attitude Structure and Change." In S. Koch (Ed.), *Psychology: A Study of Science.* Vol. 3: *Formulations of the Person and the Social Context.* New York: McGraw-Hill, 1959.

KELLEY, N. E. "A Comparative Study of Professionally Related Learning Projects of Secondary School Teachers." Master's thesis, Cornell University, 1976.

KIDD, J. R. *How Adults Learn.* New York: Association Press, 1973.

KIDD, J. R. "Adult Learning in the 1970's." In R. M. Smith (Ed.), *Adult Learning: Issues and Innovations.* Dekalb, Ill.: ERIC Clearinghouse in Career Education, 1976.

KLEIN, D. E. "Some Notes on the Dynamics of Resistance." In G. Watson (Ed.), *Concepts of Social Change.* Washington, D.C.: National Training Laboratories Institute for Applied Behavioral Science, 1967.

KNOEPFLI, H. *The Origin of Women's Autonomous Learning Groups.* Unpublished doctoral dissertation, Ontario Institute for Studies in Education, University of Toronto, 1971.

KNOWLES, M. S. *The Modern Practice of Education: Andragogy Versus Pedagogy.* New York: Association Press, 1970.

KNOWLES, M. S. *The Adult Learner: A Neglected Species.* Houston: Gulf Publishing Company, 1973.

KNOWLES, M. S. *Self Directed Learning.* New York: Association Press, 1975.

KOENIG, K., and MC KEACHIE, W. J. "Personality and Independent Study." *Journal of Educational Psychology,* 1959, *50* (3), 132–134.

KOFFMAN, E. B. "CAI Systems that Process Natural Language." *Educational Technology,* April 1974, pp. 37–42.

KORMAN, M. "Social Stress: Ethnic Differences in Coping and Defensive Styles." *The British Journal of Social Psychiatry,* 1970, *4,* 147–154.

KOSKELA, R. N. "Theoretical and Empirical Relationships Between Cognitive Styles and Cognitive Structures." Unpublished doctoral dissertation, University of Wisconsin, 1973.

KRAMER, R. M., and SPECHT, H. (Eds.). *Readings in Community Organization Practice.* Englewood Cliffs, N.J.: Prentice-Hall, 1969.

KROEBER, T. C. "The Coping Functions of the Ego Mechanisms." In R. W. White (Ed.), *The Study of Lives.* New York: Atherton Press, 1969.

KUBLER-ROSS, E., (Ed.), *Death: The Final Stage of Growth.* New York: Spectrum Books, 1975.

LAMPL, M. "Defensiveness, Dogmatism and Self-Esteem." *Dissertation Abstracts,* 1969, *29,* 2194B.

LAMPLE-DE-GROOT, J. "On Defense and Development: Normal and Pathological." *Psychoanalytic Study of the Child,* 1957, *12,* 127–150.

LANDVOGT, P. L. "A Framework for Exploring the Adult Educator's Commitment Toward the Construct of 'Guided Learning'." Master's thesis, University of Wisconsin, 1969.

LASSEY, W. R., and FERNANDEZ, R. R. *Leadership and Social Change.* La Jolla, Calif.: University Association, 1976.

LEWIN, K. "Group Decision and Social Change." In T. M. Newcomb and E. L. Hartley (Eds.), *Readings in Social Psychology.* New York: Holt, Rinehart and Winston, 1947.

LEWIN, K. *Field Theory in Social Science.* New York: Harper & Row, 1951a.

LEWIN, K. "Selected Theoretical Papers." In D. Cartwright (Ed.), *Field Theory in Social Science.* New York: Harper & Row, 1951b.

LICHTENBERG, J., and SLAP, J. "On the Defensive Organization." *International Journal of Psychoanalysis,* 1971, *52* (4).

LINDEMAN, E. C. "The Sociology of Adult Education." *Journal of Educational Sociology,* 1945, *19,* 4–13.

LINDEMAN, E. C. *The Meaning of Adult Education.* Montreal: Harvest House, 1961.

LIPPITT, R. "Dimensions of a Consultant's Job." *Journal of Social Issues,* 1959, *15,* 5–12.

LIPPITT, R., WATSON, J., and WESTLEY, B. *The Dynamics of Planned Change.* New York: Harcourt Brace Jovanovich, 1958.

LITTLE, D. Personal interview at University of British Columbia, Vancouver, B.C., March 1977.

LITTLE, D. "Adult Learning and Education: A Conceptual Model." Paper presented at Adult Education Research Conference, San Antonio, Tex., April 1978.

LITTRELL, D. W. *The Theory and Practice of Community Development.* Columbia: Extension Division, University of Missouri, 1970.

LIVERIGHT, A. A. *Strategies of Leadership.* New York: Harper & Row, 1959.

LONDON, J. "The Social Setting of Adult Education." In R. S. Smith, G. F. Aker, and J. R. Kidd (Eds.), *Handbook of Adult Education.* New York: Macmillan, 1970.

LONG, H. B., ANDERSON, R. C., and BLUBAUGH, J. A. "Six Approaches to Community Development: An Introduction." In H. B. Long, R. C. Anderson, and J. A. Blubaugh (Eds.), *Approaches to Community Development.* Iowa City, Iowa: American College Testing Program, 1973.

LONG, N. E. "The Local Community as an Ecology of Games." *American Journal of Sociology,* 1958, *63,* 251–261.

LOOMIS, C. P. *Social Systems: Essays on Their Persistence and Change.* Princeton, N.J.: Van Nostrand, 1960.

LUFT, J. *Group Processes: An Introduction to Group Dynamics.* Palo Alto, Calif.: National Press Books, 1970.

LUIKART, C. "Social Networks and Self-Planned Adult Learning." *University of North Carolina Extension Bulletin,* 1977, *61* (entire issue).

LYMAN, E. R. *A Summary of PLATO Curriculum and Research Materials.* Urbana: University of Illinois, 1972.

LYSTAD, M. M. "Institutional Planning for Social Change." *Sociology and Social Research,* 1960, *44,* 165–171.

MC CATTY, C. "Patterns of Learning Projects Among Professional Men." Unpublished doctoral dissertation, University of Toronto, 1973.

MACCIA, E. S. "Instruction as Influence Toward Rule-Governed Behavior. In R. Hyman (Ed.), *Contemporary Thought on Teaching.* Englewood Cliffs, N.J.: Prentice-Hall, 1971.

MC CLELLAND, D. L., and OTHERS. *The Achievement Motive.* New York: Appleton-Century-Crofts, 1953.

MC CLUSKY, H. Y. "Community Development." In M. S. Knowles (Ed.), *Handbook of Adult Education in the United States.* Chicago: Adult Education Association, 1960.

MC CLUSKY, H. Y. "An Approach to a Differential Psychology of the Adult Potential." In S. M. Grabowski (Ed.), *Adult Learning and Instruction.* Syracuse, N.Y.: Clearinghouse on Adult Education and Adult Education Association, 1970.

MC CLUSKY, H. Y. "The Information Self-Help Approach." In H. B. Long, R. C. Anderson, and J. A. Blubaugh (Eds.), *Approaches to Community Development.* Iowa City, Iowa: American College Testing Program, 1973.

MAC DONALD, J. S. "Independent Learning: The Theme of the Conference." In G. T. Gleason (Ed.), *The Theory and Nature of Independent Learning.* Scranton, Pa.: International Textbook, 1967.

MC DOUGALL, W. *The Group Mind.* New York: Putnam's, 1920.

MC GUIRE, W. J. "Attitudes and Opinions." *Annual Review of Psychology,* 1966, *17,* 485.

MC KEACHIE, W. J. *New Developments in Teaching, New Dimensions in Higher Education,* No. 16. ERIC ED 013 341. Bethesda, Md.: ERIC Document Reproduction Service, 1967.

MAC KENZIE, O., CHRISTENSEN, E. L., and RIGBY, P. H. *Correspondence Instruction in The United States.* New York: McGraw-Hill, 1968.

MC KEOWN, J. E. *Economics.* Chicago: The American School, 1970.

MAC KERACHER, D., DAVIE, L., and PATTERSON, T. "Community Development: Evaluation and the Shapes Approach." *Journal of the Community Development Society,* 1976, 7 (2), 4–17.

MAGER, R. F. *Preparing Instructional Objectives.* Belmont, Calif.: Fearon, 1962.

MAIER, N. R. A. *Problem Solving Discussions and Conferences.* New York: McGraw-Hill, 1963.

MARCSON, S. "Social Change and Social Structure in Transitional Societies." *International Journal of Comparative Sociology,* 1960, *1* (2), 248–253.

MARROW, A., and FRENCH, J., JR. "Changing a Stereotype in Industry." In W. G. Bennis and others (Eds.), *The Planning of Change.* (3rd ed.) New York: Holt, Rinehart and Winston, 1961.

MASLOW, A. H. *Toward a Psychology of Being.* New York: Van Nostrand, 1962.

MASLOW, A. H. "Some Educational Implications of the Humanistic Psychologies." *Harvard Education Review,* Fall 1968, *38,* 685–696.

MASLOW, A. H. *Motivation and Personality.* New York: Harper & Row, 1970.

MATHIESON, D. E. *Correspondence Study: A Summary Review of the Research and Development Literature.* Syracuse, N.Y.: ERIC Clearing House on Adult Education, 1971.

MAY, R. *Man's Search for Himself.* New York: Dell, 1953.

MAY, R. *Psychology and the Human Dilemma.* Princeton, N.J.: Van Nostrand, 1967.

MESAROVIC, M., and MACKO, D. "Scientific Theory of Hierarchical Systems." In L. L. Whyte and others (Eds.), *Hierarchical Structures.* New York: Elsevier, 1969.

MEYERSON, R., and KATZ, E. "Notes on a Natural History of Fads." *American Journal of Sociology,* 1957, *62,* 596–600.

MICHAEL, D. N. *On Learning to Plan—and Planning to Learn: The Social Psychology of Changing Toward Future-Responsive Societal Learning.* San Francisco: Jossey-Bass, 1973.

MILLER, J. G. "Toward a General Theory for the Behavioral Sciences." *The American Psychologist,* 1955, *10.*

MINAR, D. W., and GREER, S. *The Concept of Community: Readings With Interpretations.* Chicago: Aldine, 1969.

MUNSON, B. E. *Changing Community Dimensions: The Interrelationships of Social and Economic Variables.* Columbus: Ohio State University, 1968.

MURPHY, L. "Coping Devices and Defense Mechanisms in Relation to Autonomous Ego Functions." *Bulletin Menninger Clinic,* 1960, *24,* 144–153.

NAPIER, R. W., and GERSHENFELD, M. *Groups: Theory and Experience.* Boston: Houghton Mifflin, 1973.

National University Extension Association. *Descriptive Exposition of the Independent Study Division: National University Extension Association.* Washington, D.C.: Independent Study Division, National University Extension Association, 1969.

NEILL, A. S. *Summerhill: A Radical Approach to Child Rearing.* New York: Hart, 1960.

NEUMANN, E. *The Origins and History of Consciousness.* Princeton, N.J.: Princeton University Press, 1973.

NEWCOMB, T. M. *Personality and Social Change.* New York: Dryden, 1943.

OHLIGER, J. "Adult Education 1984." In I. Lister (Ed.), *Deschooling: A Reader.* New York: Cambridge University Press, 1974a.

OHLIGER, J. "Is Lifelong Adult Education a Guaranteee of Permanent Inadequacy?" *Convergence,* 1974b, *7* (2), 52.

OHLIGER, J. "Prospects for a Learning Society." *Adult Leadership,* September 1975.

OLSON, M. *The Logic of Collective Action*. Cambridge, Mass.: Harvard University Press, 1971.

OSTROM, E., and OSTROM, V. "Theoretical Foundations for a Public Choice Approach." Bloomington: Indiana University, 1972.

OWENS, R. G., and STEINHOFF, C. R. *Administering Change in Schools*. Englewood Cliffs, N.J.: Prentice-Hall, 1976.

PARSONS, T. *The Social System*. New York: Free Press, 1951.

PAULSON, B., and HARPOLE, R. "The New Community as an Application of Community Health." Paper presented at annual meeting of Adult Education Association, Atlanta, 1970.

PENLAND, P. R. "Individual Self-Planned Learning in America." Pittsburgh: Graduate School of Library and Information Sciences, University of Pittsburgh, 1977. (Available from the University of Pittsburgh Bookstore under the title *Self-Planned Learning in America;* will soon be available from ERIC.)

PERRY, W. *Open University: A Personal Account by the First Vice Chancellor Walter Perry*. Milton Keynes, England: Open University Press, 1976.

PETERS, J. M., and GORDON, S. *Adult Learning Projects: A Study of Adult Learning in Urban and Rural Tennessee*. ERIC ED 102 431. Knoxville: University of Tennessee, 1974.

PIAGET, J. *The Construction of Reality in the Child*. New York: Basic Books, 1954.

PIAGET, J. *The Psychology of Intelligence*. Paterson, N.J.: Littlefield, Adams, 1960.

PINE, G. J., and HORNE, P. J. "Principles and Conditions for Learning in Adult Education." *Adult Leadership*, October 1969, *18*, 109–110.

POSTON, R. W. "The Relationship of Community Development to Adult Education." *Adult Education*, 1954, *4* (6), 191–196.

POWER, H. "Education for Social and Public Responsibility." In R. M. Smith, G. F. Aker, and J. R. Kidd, (Eds.), *Handbook of Adult Education*. New York: Macmillan, 1970.

PRIDHAM, K. F. "Stress-Resolving Moves in an Adult Instructional Small Group." Unpublished doctoral dissertation, University of Wisconsin, 1972.

PYLE, H. G. In Stanley Drazek (Ed.), *Exploring Horizons . . . Continuing Education; The Golden Anniversary Publication of the NUEA*.

Washington, D.C.: National University Extension Association, 1965.

REDL, F. "Group Emotion and Leadership." *Psychiatry*, 1942, *5*, 573–596.

RIESMAN, D. *Individualism Reconsidered.* New York: Free Press, 1954.

ROBINSON, R. D. "Toward a Conceptualization of Leadership for Change." *Adult Education*, 1970, *20* (3), 131–139.

ROBINSON, R. D. "A Study of the Effect of Television Combined with Discussion Groups and Study Materials on the Changing of Attitudes on Social Issues." ERIC ED 049 415. Paper presented at Adult Education Research Conference, New York City, Feb. 1971.

ROBINSON, R. D., and SPAIGHTS, E. "A Study of Attitudinal Change Through Lecture Discussion Workshops." *Adult Education*, 1969, *29* (3), 163–171.

ROGERS, C. *On Becoming a Person.* Boston: Houghton Mifflin, 1961.

ROGERS, C. *Client-Centered Therapy.* Boston: Houghton Mifflin, 1965.

ROGERS, C. *Freedom to Learn.* Columbus, Ohio: Merrill, 1969.

ROGERS, E. M., and SHOEMAKER, F. F. *Communication of Innovations.* New York: Free Press, 1971.

ROGGE, W. "Independent Study is Self-Directed Learning." In D. Beggs and E. Buffie (Eds.), *Independent Study: Bold New Venture.* Bloomington: Indiana University Press, 1965.

ROKEACH, M. *The Open and Closed Mind.* New York: Basic Books, 1960.

ROSENTHAL, R., and JACOBSON, L. *Pygmalion in the Classroom.* New York: Holt, Rinehart and Winston, 1968.

ROSS, R., and STAINES, G. L. "The Politics of Analyzing Social Problems," *Social Problems*, 1972, *20*, 18–40.

ROTHMAN, J. "Three Models of Community Organization Practice." In F. M. Cox and others (Eds.), *Strategies of Community Organization: A Book of Readings.* (2nd ed.) Itasca, Ill.: Peacock, 1974.

SARBIN, T. R. "Role Theory." In G. Lindzey (Ed.), *Handbook of Social Psychology.* Cambridge, Mass.: Addison-Wesley, 1966.

SCHEIN, E. R., and BENNIS, W. G. *Personal and Organizational Change Through Group Methods.* New York: Wiley, 1965.

SCHILLER, M. "Ego Strength, Manifest Anxiety, and Defensiveness." Master's thesis, Michigan State University, 1958.

SCHLESINGER, H. "Cognitive Attitudes in Relation to Susceptibility to Interference." *Journal of Personality*, 1954, *22*, 354–374.

SCHMUCK, R. A., and SCHMUCK, P. A. *Group Processes in the Classroom.* Dubuque, Iowa: Wm. C. Brown, 1971.

SCHON, D. A. *Technology and Change.* New York: Delacorte Press, 1967.

SCHON, D. A. "Deutero-Learning in Organizations: Learning for Increased Effectiveness." *Organizational Dynamics*, Summer 1975, pp. 2–16.

SCHROEDER, W. L. "Adult Education Defined and Described." In R. M. Smith, G. F. Aker, and J. R. Kidd (Eds.), *Handbook of Adult Education.* New York: Macmillan, 1970.

SCHUTZ, W. *The Interpersonal Underworld.* Palo Alto, Calif.: Science & Behavior Books, 1970.

SEASHORE, S. E. *Group Cohesiveness in the Industrial Work Group.* Ann Arbor: University of Michigan, 1954.

SEEMAN, M. "Powerlessness and Knowledge: A Comparative Study of Alienation and Learning." *Sociometry*, 1967, *30*, 105–123.

SELLER, M. "Success and Failure in Adult Education: The Immigrant Experience 1914–1924." *Adult Education*, 1978, *28* (2), 83–99.

SEWELL, J. *Up Against City Hall.* Toronto: James Lewis and Samuel, 1972.

SHAW, M. E. *Group Dynamics: The Psychology of Small Group Behavior.* New York: McGraw-Hill, 1971.

SHEATS, P. "Introduction." In R. S. Smith, G. F. Aker, and J. R. Kidd (Eds.), *Handbook of Adult Education.* New York: Macmillan, 1970.

SIEBER, S. D. "Organizational Resistance to Innovative Roles in Educational Organization." New York: Bureau of Applied Social Research, Columbia University, 1967.

SIMON, S. B., HOWE, L., and KIRSCHENBAUM, H. *Values Clarification: A Handbook of Practical Strategies for Teachers and Students.* New York: Hart, 1972.

SIROKA, R. W., SIROKA, E. K., and SCHLOSS, G. A. (Eds.). *Sensitivity Training and Group Encounter.* New York: Grosset and Dunlap, 1971.

SIVATKO, J. R. "Correspondence Instruction." In R. Ebel (Ed.), *En-*

cyclopedia of Educational Research. (4th ed.) New York: Macmillan, 1969.

SKINNER, B. F. *The Technology of Teaching.* New York: Appleton-Century-Crofts, 1968.

SLATER, P. E. "Role Differentiation in Small Groups." *American Sociology Review,* 1955, *20,* 300–310.

SLATER, P. E. *Microcosm.* New York: Wiley, 1966.

SMITH, B. O. "A Concept of Teaching." *Teachers College Record,* February 1960, *61,* 229–241.

SMITH, R. M., AKER, G. F., and KIDD, J. R., (Eds.). *Handbook of Adult Education.* New York: Macmillan, 1970.

SORBER, E. R. *Individualization of Instruction for Teacher Corpsmen.* ERIC ED 026 341. Bethesda, Md.: ERIC Document Reproduction Service, 1968.

SORK, T. J. "Identifying Community Educational Needs or Is There a Doctor in the House?" *Adult Leadership,* May 1977, *25* (9), 277.

SOROKIN, P. *Society, Culture, and Personality.* New York: Harper & Row, 1947.

SPENCE, K. W. *Behavior Theory & Learning.* Englewood Cliffs, N.J.: Prentice-Hall, 1960.

STEELE, S. M. *Contemporary Approaches to Program Evaluation: Implications for Disadvantaged Adults.* Washington, D.C.: Educational Resources Division, Capital Publications, 1973.

STOCK, D., and THELEN, H. A. *Emotional Dynamics and Group Culture: Experimental Studies of Individual and Group Behavior.* New York: New York University Press, 1958.

SUTTON, W. A. "The Sociological Implications of the Community Development Process." In L. J. Cary (Ed.), *Community Development as a Process.* Columbia: University of Missouri Press, 1970.

THELEN, H. A. "Work-Emotionality Theory of the Group as Organism." In Koch (Ed.), *Psychology: A Study of a Science.* Vol. 3. New York: McGraw-Hill, 1959.

THELEN, H. A. *Dynamics of Groups at Work.* Chicago: University of Chicago Press, 1968.

THELEN, H. A. *Education and the Human Quest.* Chicago: University of Chicago Press, 1972.

THEODORSON, G. A., and THEODORSON, A. G. *A Modern Dictionary of Sociology.* New York: Crowell, 1969.

THORNDIKE, E. L. *Selected W⸺ings from a Correctionists Psychology.* New York: Appleton-Century-Crofts, 1949.

TOUGH, A. *Learning Without a Teacher: A Study of Tasks and Assistance During Adult Self-Teaching Projects.* Toronto: Ontario Institute for Studies in Education, 1967.

TOUGH, A. *The Adult's Learning Projects: A Fresh Approach to Theory and Practice in Adult Learning.* Toronto: Ontario Institute for Studies in Education, 1971.

TUCKER, D. M. "Some Relationships Between Individual and Group Development." *Human Development,* 1973, *16,* 249–272.

TUCKMAN, B. W. "Developmental Sequence in Small Groups." *Psychological Bulletin,* 1965, *63,* 384–395.

TWYFORD, L. C., JR. "Educational Communications Media." In R. Ebel (Ed.), *Encyclopedia of Educational Research.* (4th ed.) New York: Macmillan, 1969.

VALLEY, J. "Diversity Plus 2." *The College Board Review,* Summer 1975, *96,* 17–21, 31–32.

VERNER, C. "Definition of Terms." In G. Jensen, A. A. Liveright, and W. Hallenback (Eds.), *Adult Education: Outlines of an Emerging Field of University Study.* Washington, D.C.: Adult Education Association, 1964.

WALZTAWICK, P., BEAVIN, J. H., and JACKSON, D. D. *Pragmatics of Human Communication.* New York: Norton, 1967.

WARREN, R. *The Community in America.* Chicago: Rand McNally, 1972.

WATSON, G. *Social Psychology: Issues and Insights.* Philadelphia: Lippincott, 1966.

WAXLER, N. "Defense Mechanisms and Interpersonal Anxiety." Unpublished doctoral dissertation, Harvard University, 1960.

WEDEMEYER, C. A. "New Uses for the 'Tools' of Education." *The NUEA Spectator,* April–May 1965, *30,* 14–19, 25.

WEDEMEYER, C. A. "Independent Study." In L. C. Deighton (Ed.), *The Encyclopedia of Education.* Vol. 4. New York: Macmillan, 1971.

WEISMAN, H., RITTER, K., and GORDON, R. "Reliability of the Defense Mechanisms Inventory." *Psychological Reports,* 1971, *29* (3), 1237–1238.

"What is Adult Education? Nine 'Working Definitions'." *Adult Education,* 1955, *5,* 131–145.

WHITE, R. "Ego and Reality in Psychoanalytic Theory." *Psychological Issues,* 1963, *3* (3), 39.

WHITE, S. W. "The Relationship of Small Group Members' Ego-Identity Concerns and Their Employment of Mechanisms of Coping and Defense." Unpublished doctoral dissertation, University of Wisconsin, 1976.

WHITNEY, V. H. "Resistance to Innovations: The Case of Atomic Power." *American Journal of Sociology,* 1950, *56,* 247–254.

WILEDEN, A. F. *Community Development.* Totowa, N.J.: Bedminster Press, 1970.

WILKINSON, K. P. "The Community as a Social Field." *Social Forces,* 1970.

WILKINSON, K. P. "A Field-Theory Perspective for Community Development Research." *Rural Sociology,* 1972.

WILSON, J. P. "Coping-Defense Employment in Small Groups." *Small Group Behavior,* 1977, *9* (2).

WILSON, S. P. "The Relationship Between Compatibility of Ego Identity Concerns Among Dyad Members and Employment of Coping-Defense Mechanisms in Problem Solving Situations." Unpublished doctoral dissertation, University of Wisconsin, 1973.

WINNER, L. *Autonomous Technology: Technics-out-of-Control as a Theme in Political Thought.* Cambridge, Mass.: M.I.T. Press, 1977.

WITKIN, H. A., and OTHERS. *Psychological Differentiation.* New York: Wiley, 1962.

WITKIN, H. A., and OTHERS. "Field-Dependent and Field-Independent Cognitive Styles and Their Educational Implications." *Review of Educational Research,* 1977, *47* (1), 1–64.

WOODRUFF, A. D. "Cognitive Models of Learning & Instruction." In L. Siegel (Ed.), *Instruction: Some Contemporary Viewpoints.* San Francisco: Chandler, 1967.

YEAZELL, M. I. "Theory and Practice: Innovations in Teaching Educational Psychology." *The Journal of Teacher Education,* Winter 1971, *22,* 412–417.

ZIEGLER, W. L. "On Civic Literacy." Syracuse, N.Y.: Educational Policy Research Corporation, 1974.

Index